Charles Carter

8826 James Rd. S.W

Rochester
Wash.

Something Worse Than Hell
and Better Than Heaven

by Jerry Barnard
with Don Tanner and Bruce Anderson

Published by
Hunter Books
1602 Townhurst
Houston, Texas 77043

Books by Jerry Barnard

Something Worse Than Hell
   and Better Than Heaven
Turn Loose, the Jerry Barnard Story

Record Albums/Cassettes/8 Tracks

I'll See You in The Rapture
Most Requested Hymns
It's Real
Just A Preacher

Scripture quotations are taken from the King James Version.

Jerry Barnard may be contacted through Faith Outreach International, P.O. Box 413, San Diego, CA 92112.

ISBN 0-917726-31-6

FOREWORD

We probably would never have discovered the better-than-heaven joys and the agony of worse-than-hell torments if we hadn't read this book. What an eye-opener it has been!

It will challenge the silence many Christians maintain around others and it will bring into focus the flimsiness of excuses which are offered for shunning God.

Many people say, "I don't want to go to heaven. I want to go to hell so I'll be with my friends," without realizing what they are saying. This book will make those words choke right in your throat if you've ever said them. And when the realization comes that we could even be responsible for something worse than hell, it makes us want to get up on more soap boxes than we've already been on, and shout louder than ever before about God's wonderful love.

Even though we are made in God's image, we will never understand him, but we don't have to. All we need to remember is that he loves us and he wants us, and his desire is that none of us should perish. Many of our friends and loved ones can join with us on that great day if we will just share with them the glorious and endless love of God. To try to understand the joy we'll feel when we get to heaven and see something better than heaven is an overwhelming thought!

Whether you're saved or unsaved, you'll love every single word in this book because it will steal people right out of the pits of hell and deposit them in the arms of God!

Charles and Frances Hunter

DEDICATED TO
those who have given this book personal warmth
by sharing their trials and triumphs

Contents

Introduction

CHAPTER 1

ARE WE ALONE?

"You have the absolute right to remain silent. Anything you say can and will be used against you in a court of law . . . ."

Like the fury of fire, the agony of these words tormented Gary Jacobs as he sat pensively on the edge of the narrow, cold cot in his scant cell. Nine years after joining the San Diego Police Department, Officer Jacobs now pondered his future from the wrong side of the prison bars.

His life had been comfortable — nice house and cars, a boat, horses, recreational vehicles. The family never lacked money, for in addition to his policeman's salary, Gary ran two businesses on the side; a trucking firm and a tool parts store.

That was where the trouble came. His partner in the parts store had found a source of good tools for unusually low prices. Although Gary had been suspicious about the deal, he decided not to look into it. Later he discovered, to his dismay, that the tools were being stolen from the government.

Eventually, catching on to the scheme, police detectives followed the supplier to the parts store, where Gary and his partner were arrested.

Held in solitary confinement for protection because he was a police officer, Gary endured an eight week trial before a hostile judge. His bitterness at what he felt was an unjust imprisonment was heightened by the fact that his partner, who had solely arranged the transaction, was released without trial.

After the jury brought in a verdict of guilty, Gary was released on bail until the sentencing date.

"You have a clean record," his lawyers comforted. "The judge will probably give you a three month suspended sentence or probation."

The probation department recommended no jail time. The prosecuting attorney asked for thirty days at most. Gary's heart sank when the stern judge handed down the sentence: "One year in jail and three years' probation."

Returned to solitary confinement, Gary sat idly day after day in a five by ten foot cell, waiting for word on his appeal for a transfer to the honor camp. Without windows, time had no signposts. Days lost their dawning, nights their sunset. Within him, depression introduced a strange new cellmate. Offering fascinating promises of escape, suicide would have claimed a new victim were it not for the words of an invisible Friend. Day after day, Gary thumbed through a copy of the Bible left in his cell, praying constantly to a God he hoped was listening.

"God, why don't you let me out of jail?" he demanded. "Why must I go crazy in solitary confinement? Why can't I go to the honor camp?"

Soon after, the clanking of keys announced the visit of an official in charge of the camps. "You're leaving for honor camp tomorrow," he announced.

Surprised, Gary made no reply. Staring at the ceiling, he was now certain that God had heard his prayers.

"It felt like warm water pouring down over my body," Gary recalls. "I didn't hear anything or see any lights, but I'm convinced the answer was from above."

Gary spent the next thirty days working in the kitchen at the honor camp before he was enrolled in a work furlough program.

During that month, a fellow prisoner loaned him a copy of my biography, Turn Loose. He had read a few similar books before, but parts of this one struck home. Gary identified with my desires for the good life and the arguments I had with God over my entering the ministry. Although I eventually yielded to God's call, my struggles intrigued him, and he wanted to meet me. His requests to have me speak at the honor camp were denied by the prison authorities, but Gary and a few others were allowed to watch religious programs on television. One of the telecasts they viewed was the Sharing With Jerry Barnard Program. The relationship between God and me,

which was projected on that series, deepened
Gary's interest in meeting me.

A Surprising Turn

A few months later, Gary was up for parole.
The papers had easily gone through the parole
board. Gary's wife, Peggy, wrote a long letter to
the judge about her plight: Their boy was seri-
ously ill, the family was on welfare, the house had
been flooded, later it had been attacked by a
gang, which she had driven off by gunfire. Surely
"His Honor" would release him for these reasons,
Gary reasoned.

But with a look that Gary interpreted as pure
hatred, the magistrate abruptly denied his release.
Hopes dashed, Gary returned to the honor camp.

"Why, God?" he demanded bitterly. "Peggy is
scared to death, and I learned my lesson on Day
One in jail. Why can't I be released?"

A month went by without an answer, when
suddenly the judge called him back. Thinking one
of his attorneys had arranged the meeting, Gary
was bewildered when he learned the official had
initiated the review.

As he walked into the room, Gary realized im-
mediately that his prayers had been answered.
Once full of contempt for a police officer in-
volved in crime, the judge was now smiling and
speaking kindly to Gary for the first time. The
constant prayers of his wife, her aunt, his fellow
prisoners who were Christians, and many others
had been answered. The attorneys stared at the

judge in disbelief, not understanding his change in attitude. It had to be a miracle. To this they agreed as Gary went home a free man.

The week after his release, Gary and his wife visited our Sunday service. Nervously they sat and listened to the sermon.

I had planned to skip the usual invitation for those who wanted to give their lives to Christ to come forward, but a divine voice inside insisted I make the request. As the call went forth, Gary and Peggy sprang to their feet. Neither one had discussed salvation with the other, but both responded simultaneously. In a moment, each made a public confession of Jesus as Savior, and the months of bitterness melted away. The couple began a new life of joy that Sunday morning.

Gary has since found a job. His son, Wesley, was miraculously healed of kidney disease, and Gary's life now has new purpose.

"I couldn't ask for anything more," he smiles. "I've still got a lot of bills to pay, but I'm not worried about them. I know God will take care of us."

"Before, I never wanted to talk about religion because so many people are funny about it, but now I'd stand up in a crowd of atheists and tell them exactly what happened to me."

No One An Island

"No man is an island, entire of itself," the great poet John Donne wrote. Although we may not be aware of it, our lives constantly influence the

destiny of those around us. How could I know
that events from my life recorded in a book
would profoundly influence the future of an im-
prisoned policeman whom I had never met?

All of our lives are open books, being read
daily by friends and strangers. It is utterly impos-
sible to leave people exactly the way we find
them; either we add to their life or take some-
thing away. Because of us, they will never be the
same.

Our lives are pervaded by influences; some for
good, others for evil. Many reflect the love of
God in everything they do, creating peace amid
strife, goodness in the presence of evil, and joy in
the face of sorrow. Without uttering a word, they
leave everyone they meet a little happier. Others
sow seeds of dissension. Full of bitterness and
fear, they infect those about them with the
deadly virus of misery.

A Christian's influence carries with it a heavy
responsibility. People cannot see God, but they
do observe those who claim to be His followers.
Having little interest in reading the Bible, non-
believers are experts at reading Christians and al-
most invariably can distinguish between hypoc-
risy and genuine faith.

God uses three ways to touch our world: His
Spirit, His Word and His people. Of these, God's
people often are the greatest means of contact. If
those who do not know God are to hear from
Heaven, it must be through the living witness of
Heaven's ambassadors.

A World of Influences

In a world full of influences, a nudge toward God at just the right time can be crucial. Jane Buckmeier was tossed by many pressures as she battled seemingly insurmountable problems. Married to a Navy submarine technician stationed in Honolulu, Jane experienced increasing family tensions. The oldest of her seven children, Kathy, began taking drugs and running away. Jane and her husband argued constantly. Although raised in the church in Ireland, she knew little of Jesus.

Following the advice of a counselor, the Buckmeiers visited a psychiatrist, who led them into astrology. Her husband left the Navy in an attempt to solve their problems, and the couple moved to San Diego. There they had great difficulty finding a place to live, now that their family had increased.

Their daughter, Kathy, soon discovered she had a severe spine disease. As their marriage continued to deteriorate, the Buckmeiers went to a religious counseling center.

"I see little hope for you," the counselor shook his head slowly. "Your husband doesn't place his faith in God."

As Jane stood to leave, only one course seemed possible. A short time later, the couple separated.

The prospects of peace and a warm family life finally lured Jane into a religious cult. This, too, ended in disappointment. In despair she drove to the middle of the Coronado Bridge, intending to jump off. Her lone figure barely visible in the

early morning fog, Jane gripped the railing until
her knuckles turned white. She felt a strange pull
toward the icy waters far below.

"N . . . n . . . no! I can't," she stammered, bolt-
ing toward her car. As she sped erratically toward
Coronado Island, her tires vibrated with the
bump-bump-bump of the lane dividers.

Pregnant with her tenth child and in deepened
anxiety, Jane turned to a neighbor who had
shown her kindness. She readily accepted her in-
vitation to visit church. Kathy's spine was miracu-
lously healed during the service she and Jane
attended. The operation was canceled, opening a
new door of hope in the family. Jane tells the
story from this point:

> "I came back to the church the next
> week. The love the people showed me
> when I went in, shaking hands at the
> door and putting their arms around me,
> made me feel like I was really human.
> It just kept me going until the next
> week.
>
> The third Sunday, I spoke to Pastor
> Barnard. He told me no matter what
> my husband did, I should love him and
> keep showing that love. Now I had a
> goal because I had never been around
> Christian people with this kind of love
> before. Something beautiful was hap-
> pening in my life."

Despite frequent illness, Jane did not miss a
Sunday in church and soon committed her life to
Christ. Supernatural love toward her husband and

children replaced the self pity and hatred that had filled her heart. Before long, her husband noticed the change.

"After all the things I've done to you, I don't see how you could still love me," he marvelled. "If Jesus gives you that kind of love, I want to meet Him, too!"

Through Jane's influence, her husband and children surrendered to Christ. The Buckmeiers' marriage has been healed, and many of their friends have come to God. Jane recently made a pilgrimage to Ireland to witness to her family and friends. As a result of her testimony, 160 persons accepted Christ as Savior.

God's Accidents

Sometimes God uses the most unexpected people to draw others to Him. Jenny Dyer had been married for three years, and her husband, Mike, was at sea with the Navy. Both were concerned about the problems in their marriage.

Through an "accidental" mix-up in their payroll checks, Jenny and Connie Valois met and became friends. Connie lived a happy life, and Jenny was irresibly drawn toward her.

Although Jenny had been raised in church, she hadn't found anything in it to fill the emptiness she felt inside. Connie had a happiness she wanted, so Jenny began attending Christian Faith Centre with her. Fearing Mike's reaction, she did not make a commitment to Christ. Eventually, her fears proved justified. In a letter to her husband, Jenny mentioned her interest in God.

"I don't want a Jesus freak for a wife!" Mike exploded when he read the letter. He knew Robin Rambeck, a fellow seaman on the ship, was a Christian.

"Hey, Rob! Let me borrow your Bible for awhile," Mike asked one day. A self-proclaimed atheist, he hoped to find ways to disprove every principle in it to his wife. But as he read, the truth of God's Word penetrated his life, and through Robin's prayerful witness Mike gave his heart to Christ.

Weeks later when Mike arrived home on leave, Jenny knew instantly that something was different about him. They were silent on their way home from the base, even though they hadn't seen each other in seven months. Neither knew how to break the news of a new life in Jesus.

Finally, Mike broke the silence. "Jenny, I've become a Christian," he blurted just as he turned into the driveway of their home. The car stopped, and Mike turned slowly to look at his pretty young wife, whom he dearly loved. He sent up a silent prayer, "Please, Jesus, help us."

Staring at him in shock, Jenny seemed unable to grasp his words.

"I've become a Christian," he repeated, taking her by the hand. "And I love you even more."

Astounded by the great change in her husband's life, Jenny broke into sobs of joy.

"Oh, Jenny, could we just pray together. I don't know what else to say."

"Yes, Mike, we may. I'd really like to know Jesus, too."

As they prayed, Jenny committed her life to Christ.

Thousands of miles apart, they had been inspired separately by Christian friends; friends God used to heal their lives and marriage. Mike and Jenny attended Christian Faith Centre for several years before leaving for Bible college. They have since influenced many for Christ.

Reaching the Unreachable

Jackie and Doug Barlow seemed unreachable by Christian influence. In the occult for more than twenty years, Jackie was a proficient medium, practicing astrology, ESP and occultic out-of-body travel. Doug was more interested in drinking. Hardly a day went by without his consuming two six-packs of beer and a bottle of hard liquor.

A Christian neighbor talked with them about God every time she could and was even there when they took out the trash. They did their best to avoid the sermons, finally resorting to emptying their trash can in the middle of the night. Then another woman warned Jackie that her occult activities were contrary to the Bible. Before long, though not knowing these Christians were praying, she began to feel uneasy about her occult meetings.

One day as their wedding anniversary approached, Doug asked, "Honey, what would you like this year for your gift?"

"I'd like to go to church!" she blurted.

Having never attended church, both were stunned at this request.

"Where do you want to go?" Doug frowned. "We don't know of any churches."

Remembering the woman who had told her about the Bible, Jackie replied, "There's a church in San Diego I've heard about and I'd like to go there."

"Well, okay," he sighed. Since the city was sixty five miles away, Doug was certain this would be a one-time visit.

As I spoke that Sunday morning, Jackie was ready to run out, yet felt fastened to the chair. She told me later, "Pastor Barnard, you were saying things I had never heard in all my life. I didn't want to listen, yet I was curious. Most of all, you told how much God loved me and that Jesus died for Me — Jackie."

When I invited those who wanted to accept Jesus to come forward, Jackie pushed her husband out of the way to get to the front. "She's nuts," Doug muttered. Yet something strange tugged within him, and he reluctantly joined his wife at the altar. After repeating a prayer for salvation with the others, Doug sighed, "What a relief; that's over. Now I can get out of here and go have another beer!"

After that, things changed so drastically that by the end of the month, Doug hated to come home. Jackie's smile nearly drove him crazy. He no longer felt comfortable in her presence. She was a different person.

When he lost his job, she smiled undisturbed.

When he got it back, she beamed, "Thank the Lord."

When he was arrested for drunk driving, she bailed him out smiling all the while. Feeling pangs of guilt, Doug reluctantly agreed to attend a water baptismal service at the ocean with Jackie the morning after his release.

"But I certainly won't be baptized with you!" he asserted. "These people are crazy. I've always let you do as you pleased about spiritual things. I'll just go to watch."

Again, the smile flashed.

The next morning, head aching and eyes bloodshot, to please Jackie, Doug found himself walking into the ocean that cold, rainy day to be baptized. In describing what he experienced, Doug later said, "The few seconds I was under that water my whole life passed before me. All the ugly filth was being washed away. A love came over me which I cannot explain, filling me so full I thought I would burst. I just knew everything had changed."

"When I came up out of the water, it was as if I had just been born. Everything was different. I felt new, clean, beautiful. Jesus came into my life. God did for me in a few seconds what I had tried without success to do for thirty three years."

Many years have passed, and the Barlows are using their influence for God. Jackie purchased a citizens band radio and holds Bible classes each

night on the air. Several have heard the message
of Jesus, and many are accepting Christ as their
Savior over the two-way radio.

Living Monuments

Whether or not one is a Christian, each of us
influences lives around us. As our brief earthly
existence passes from the sunrise of childhood to
the sunset of old age, we set tides in motion
which continue to move through future genera-
tions.

We all are eternal monuments to good or evil,
living books read by everyone we meet. The
destiny of others depends on us. How we use our
lives has eternal consequences. It is a responsibil-
ity none can escape. We are accountable before
God for the influence we have on the people
around us. God says:

> "When I say unto the wicked, Thou
> shalt surely die; and thou givest him
> not warning, nor speakest to warn the
> wicked from his wicked way, to save
> his life; the same wicked man shall die
> in his iniquity; but his blood will I re-
> quire at thine hand.
>
> Yet if thou warn the wicked, and he
> turn not . . . from his wicked way, he
> shall die in his iniquity; but thou has
> delivered thy soul.
>
> Again, when a righteous man doth
> turn from his righteousness, and com-
> mit iniquity . . . he shall die: because

thou hast not given him warning, he
shall die in his sin . . . but his blood will
I require at thine hand.

Nevertheless, if thou warn the righ-
teous man . . . and he doth not sin, he
shall surely live, because he is warned;
also thou hast delivered thy soul."[1]

Because of this, there remains for each of us
something even better than the glories of Heaven,
yet far worse than the torments of Hell.

CHAPTER 2

A WORLD BELOW

During World War II, 700,000 Jews — men, women and children — were herded like cattle into trains and transported to Treblinka, Poland. Undressed and taken to a room for what they thought was a shower, they were exterminated by poison gas.

Christians behind the Iron Curtain suffer unspeakable tortures for their faith. "All the biblical descriptions of Hell and the pains of Dante's Inferno are nothing in comparison with the tortures in a Communist prison," says Richard Wurmbrand, one who suffered fourteen years for his faith.[1] Most stories of Communist torture cannot be told, for they are too gruesome to print. But accounts of starvation, beatings and naked exposure to extreme cold are common.

One need not look at the infamous past nor into the dungeons of oppression to see the faces of Hell. Evidence of man's misery and agony can be found even in the mansions of the world's elite. While most will agree there is a hell on Earth, they gasp in startling unbelief at the idea of a Hell in the hereafter.

"A God of love send people to Hell? Never!"
they exclaim. But if God, who is alive now, is
allowing "hell" to exist in the present, why
wouldn't He extend it into eternity?

Glimpses Beyond

In recent times, some have caught glimpses of a
horrifying nether realm through God-given visions
and trips in spirit. Their testimony leaves no
doubt that such a place exists. One account is
given by Lorne Fox, a respected missionary evan-
gelist of a major denomination. He was escorted
on his journey downward by an angel of God.

"At first, everything was clothed in
total darkness, and then after a time
there began to be faint, weird lights and
shadows, like flickering firelight, which
gradually became brighter.

At this point, the atmosphere, which
had been warm, became stifling, finally
almost unbearable . . .

Far below us, beings now began to
take a definite form. There appeared a
huge orb or sphere, which was bathed
in flames of liquid fire. At closer prox-
imity, the sphere was so large that it
was impossible to begin to see around
it. This had been the source of mysteri-
ous firelight . . .

I heard the voices of lost souls lifted
in cries, shrieks and curses. Somehow, I

knew fully that those were the realms which we speak of here on Earth as Hell . . .

I saw fear in Hell such as I have never witnessed on Earth. I have seen tragedy strike during the years of my ministry on Earth. I have seen faces blanched with terror. But I saw this thing magnified one thousand fold in the corridors of Hell. I heard anguished cries of fear! I saw the terrorized souls of the lost, trying desperately, to lose themselves in the shadows . . . but to no avail. They were always running from some enemy that did not pursue." [2]

Our only completely reliable authority on the afterworld is the Bible. A fine line exists between illusion and reality in the spirit realm where the possibility of deception is great. Therefore all eyewitness accounts of life beyond death must be judged by God's Word.

The Bible repeatedly affirms the existence of literal Hell. Jesus accepted it as fact and so did the demons He cast out. The visions of Heaven and Hell experienced by our contemporaries can be taken as important insights into eternal truth when their accounts harmonize with biblical truth, though they can never be accepted on the same level as scripture.

Another who viewed the horrors of the world below is actor Curt Jurgens. Undergoing a dangerous heart operation in Houston, Texas, he experienced the dreadful atmosphere while his body lay on the operating table. Here is his account:

"A fiery rain was now falling, but though the drops were enormous, none of them touched me. They splattered down around me, and out of them grew menacing tongues of flames licking up about me.

I could no longer shut out the frightful truth: beyond doubt the faces dominating this fiery world were faces of the damned. I had a feeling of despair . . . The sensation of horror was so great it choked me.

Obviously I was in Hell itself, and the glowing tongues of fire could be reaching me any minute."[3]

Dr. Richard Eby, a respected gynecologist and osteopath, had a two-minute vision of Hell while standing in Lazarus' tomb during a 1977 tour of Israel of which I was a part. He described the terrifying isolation and oppressive darkness of the Pit, seemingly penned in on all sides by a cold silence:

"With terror came anger: Hell-inspired curses flowed out in silence. My lips were silenced! Hate, wrath, cruelty, and insane rage rolled back and forth through me. Despite the utter silence, I heard demons taunt me: Damn God! Damn people! Damn everything! Damn me! Especially damn Jesus for doing this to me when I hadn't done anything to Him . . . In fact I had always left Him totally alone! Damn

Satan, too, the dirty deceiver. He should burn for this!"[4]

The agonies of Hell also were vividly experienced by George Godkin of Alberta, Canada:

"The darkness of Hell is so intense that it seems to have a pressure per square inch. It is an extremely black, dismal, desolate, heavy, pressurized type of darkness. It gives the individual a crushing, despondent feeling of loneliness.

The heat is a dry, dehydrating type. Your eyeballs are so dry they feel like red hot coals in their sockets. Your tongue and lips are parched and cracked with the intense heat. The breath from your nostrils as well as the air you breathe feels like a blast from a furnace. The exterior of your body feels as though it were encased within a white hot stove. The interior of your body has a sensation of scorching hot air being forced through it.

The agony and loneliness of Hell cannot be expressed clearly enough for proper understanding to the human soul; it has to be experienced."[5]

Agreeing with these descriptions is Marietta Davis, who as a young woman in the mid-1800s had visions of both Heaven and Hell. Entering the nether world in spirit form, she experienced many horrors:

"As I advanced, I walked as upon scorpions, and trod as amid living

embers. The trees that seemed to wave
about me were fiery exhaltations, and
their blossoms the sparklings and the
burnings of unremitting flames. Each
object I approached by contact created
agony.

The phosphorescent glare that sur-
rounded the various objects burned the
eye that looked upon them. The fruit
burned the hand that plucked and the
lips that received it. The gathered
flowers had emitted a burning exhalta-
tion, whose fetid and noisome odor
caused excruciating pain."[6]

As a young man, evangelist Kenneth Hagin
had a chilling battle with the nether world. With
barely enough time to say "goodbye" to
those about his death bed, Hagin's spirit rushed
from his body and sped down, down, down until
the lights of Earth faded away. Here are excerpts
from his frightening account:

The further down I went the blacker
it became, until it was all blackness. I
could not have seen my hand if it had
been one inch in front of my eyes. The
further down I went, the more stifling
it became.

Finally, I could see lights flickering
way below me, then a giant orb of
flame, which drew me like a magnet at-
tracts metal. As the heat beat me in the
face, I could not take my eyes off the
orb.

Upon reaching the bottom of the pit, I had become conscious of some kind of spirit-being by my side. That creature laid his hand on my arm half-way between my shoulder and my elbow to escort me in. At that same moment, a Voice spoke, away above the blackness, above the Earth, above the heavens. It was the voice of God. And though I did not understand what He said, His voice reverberated throughout the region of the damned, shaking it like a leaf in the wind, causing that creature to lose his grip.

A power pulled me, and I retreated from the fire and from the heat, back into the shadows of the darkness. I began to ascend, until I came to the top of the pit and saw the light of Earth. I came back into that room where my body lay. I slipped right back down into it as a man slips into his trousers in the morning.[7]

Such accounts point to the dreadful reality of this realm. Indisputably stronger is the evidence given in the Bible.

Despite modern denials of Hell's existence, God's Word presents it as a literal place. In fact, Jesus made more references to the abyss than to Heaven. Passionately using every approach at His command to warn people about the lower world, Jesus offered Himself as a means for escape. "Believe on me, and you will not perish," He said. "But reject me, and you will be damned."

It would be easier to lash a stormy sea into submission with a thread, move the Rocky Mountains with a spoon or drain the ocean with a thimble than to remove Hell from the Bible. It is there because it is fact.

Jesus related the story of a rich man enduring the fires of Hell. Most theologians agree that this is a true account of a real person, not just a colorful parable. When the rich man died, he looked into Paradise and saw the wretched beggar, Lazarus, who had lain unheeded at his doorstep until he died.

"Abraham!" he cried to the Patriarch on whose bosom Lazarus lay. "I am in anguish from these flames. Send Lazarus to dip his finger in water and cool my tongue. The fire is tormenting me!"

"That's not possible," Abraham returned. "Lazarus suffered in life while you lived in comfort. Now the tables are turned. Besides, an unbridgeable chasm separates us from you."

"Then please send him to my earthly home," the rich man begged. "Ask him to warn my five brothers about this dreadful place so they won't come here too!"

"They have all the warning they need in the Scripture," Abraham replied. "If they won't listen to that, they wouldn't be impressed by someone rising from the dead."[8]

A Place of Emotion

Three aspects of this story attract my attention. The first is the emotion which gripped the

rich man. In the story he "cried and said . . . ."
One translation says, "He cried through his
tears."

However it is translated, we can be certain that
the rich man was motivated by a desperate desire
for mercy. His brief residence in Hell had
awakened all the emotions he may have felt in life,
but never expressed. Here lies the tragedy: If he
had been that emotional about his welfare on
Earth, the story could have had another ending.
Had he prayed in life with the same fervency he
prayed in Hell, his final lot would have been far
different.

Genuine emotion — deep, sincere feeling — is
an element almost entirely lost to the modern
church. It is a rare experience indeed to hear a
minister preach with such power that the audi-
ence wants to cry aloud for mercy. Those mag-
nificent words of praise which once burst spon-
taneously from grateful hearts to do works of
wonder are nearly gone from human vocabulary.
In this day of cold and formal religion, such out-
bursts are considered unseemly; anyone shouting
out the praises of God or weeping under the
weight of sin may fall prey to an usher's heavy
hand escorting him out of the service.

So often the old songs have lost their tri-
umphant ring, becoming funeral dirges. One by
one the voices of faith's staunch defenders are
stilled by death, to be replaced with the dulcet
tones of polished, professional preachers.

Failing to believe in the existence of Hell, too
many are denying even the reality of God. Mir-
acles and healing are dismissed as fantasy, the

deity of Christ as a myth. Is it any wonder many churches are losing the battle for their survival?

Yet, at the same time, a genuine renewal is touching many denominations, and God is upholding all people of faith. The sorrowing are coming to the house of God to exchange their tears for smiles of joy. The lonely are finding friendship and fellowship in the church. There are active altars on which the distressed leave their burdens. The church is again becoming vibrant with life and throbbing with power.

My heart cries out for a restoration of true emotion to all the church. I want to hear all people sing from the heart again. I want to see tears of repentance and joy, glistening like priceless pearls on the cheeks of men and women, boys and girls. I want to witness the throbbing, surging, pulsating power of the Holy Spirit operating in every place where people gather in the name of the Lord. I want every minister to be "a flame of fire,"[9] with soul ablaze for God and bearing the unquenchable torch of conquering truth.

I can assure you that the death of Jesus on Calvary was an event charged with emotion. There was nothing passive about it. When He cried, "Eloi, Eloi, Lama Sabactani – My God, My God, why hast Thou forsaken Me?" – it was from the depths of His agonizing soul. He bore the sins of the world on His lacerated back. He held the fate of mankind in His pierced hands. He was engaged in the most important and decisive battle the world has ever known, for the victory won or lost on Calvary would decide the destiny of all mankind. Jesus was fighting that desperate battle with all the power of His soul, mind and body, and He was determined to win.

We are engaged in the same kind of battle today, and nothing less than our wholehearted effort will win the victory. The world will never be won to God by half-hearted apologists or lukewarm Christians, but by dedicated men and women whose hearts are ablaze with a passion for mankind and consumed with a fervent zeal to serve God.

Why should emotion be reserved for Hell, when it is too late? Now is the time for the driving power of compassion and concern for those on the downward road to damnation. Tomorrow may be too late.

One Man's Desperate Concern

Another insight we can draw from the story of Lazarus is that the rich man in Hell had a spiritual quality sometimes difficult to find among professing Christians today. He was concerned about the destiny of others. Astonishingly, the rich man, was concerned about his brothers. His passion for their safety rose within his pain, and he begged for their salvation.

What an amazing thought! Already in Hell, he possessed what every Christian on Earth should have.

Do you care about the fate of your friends and relatives? When was the last time you bent your

knees in a prayer of intercession for them? Have
you ever made an individual the object of your
prayer and held on until that person was brought
to Christ?

Such a burning zeal for others is something you
must have if you wish to please God.

What an indictment to see a man already in
Hell, whose prayers could mean nothing, have
more compassion for his relatives than most of us
on Earth.

Speaking From Experience

This brings us to the third truth in the story:
The rich man spoke from experience. He knew
what Hell was like because he was there. The
flames of fire held him in their blazing embrace.
His soul was withering in agony and torment as he
reeled under the searing lash of memory —
thoughts of happy years which passed so swiftly
by, of bright days he supposed would never end,
of precious moments when he could have altered
his destiny with a word. But thoughtlessly he had
wasted those years, carelessly letting all those
priceless moments go by without uttering a single
prayer.

Then one dark night, death had placed its bony
hand on his shoulder. "It's time for your reckon-
ing," it sneered, wrapping skeletal fingers around
his heart and forever stilling its beat.

Suddenly, the rich man knew what Hell was
like. He understood he was eternally lost, never

again to hear the voice of God, never again to take a breath free of pain!

Whatever he had believed on Earth, he could not deny the torment that now racked his being, the thirst that seared his throat and parched his lips. The evidence came indisputably to him in the wails of other damned souls bursting endlessly upon his consciousness.

Meeting kings and thieves, he saw all of them brought together into one great chorus of agony. Yes, he certainly believed in Hell now, and he was speaking from experience.

Consider the Evidence

Why must we learn so much for ourselves? Why can't we accept the first-hand accounts of others and change before it is too late?

Hell is the final end where the streets of evil converge. A grim reality, its existence is firmly based on biblical evidence.

Called <u>Sheol</u> in the Old Testament and <u>Hades</u> in the New Testament, Hell is revealed as a place of torment, perhaps containing several compartments. The Psalmist wrote that "the wicked shall be turned into Hell (Sheol) and all the nations that forget God."[10] Job called it the "realm of the dead."[11] It is there that the angels who sinned were committed to "pits of darkness" until the judgment.[12] And it is the place where demons fear to go before their time.[13]

Although the Bible does not give a detailed portrait of Hades, it does provide a glimpse of the

torments awaiting those who persist in going
there. Some of these are listed below:

A bottomless pit	Revelation 20:1
A horrible tempest	Psalm 11:6
A furnace of fire	Matthew 13:41,42
A place of torments	Luke 16:23
A place of everlasting punishment	Matthew 25:46
A place where people pray	Luke 16:27
Where they scream for mercy	Luke 16:24
Where they wail	Matthew 13:42
Where they can never repent	Matthew 12:32
A place of filthiness	Revelation 22:10,11
A place of weeping	Matthew 8:12
A place of sorrows	Psalm 18:5
A place of outer darkness	Matthew 8:12
A place where they have no rest	Revelation 14:11
A place of blackness, or darkness forever	Jude 13
A place where their worm dieth not and fire is not quenched	Mark 9:48
A place where they will be tormented with brimstone	Revelation 14:10
A place where they will be tormented with fire	Luke 16:24
A place where they will drink the wine of God's wrath	Revelation 14:10
A place where they did not want their loved ones to come	Luke 16:28
A place of quick burning coals	Psalm 11:6
A place where they beg for water	Luke 16:24
A place of gnashing of teeth	Matthew 8:12
A place of sorcerers, amoral, murderers, idolators	Revelation 22:15

Where Is 'Below'?

Where could such a horrible place be? Some
say it is in the heart of the Earth, a molten sea of
flame at the planet's core. Others theorize it must
be a planet beyond the reach of the brightest sun,

forever enshrouded by the darkness of endless night and wrapped in the stifling mantle of eternal stillness.

Perhaps it rests in another dimension we can know nothing about in this present life.

Of one thing we can be sure: Hell is where God is not. Jesus said, "Depart from me, ye cursed, into everlasting fire, prepared for the devil and his angels."[14]

If Hell is on an earthly dimension, the Bible indicates it is "down" or "beneath," while Heaven is always "up." At His death, Jesus went "into the heart of the Earth" to preach to the captive spirits.[15]

For rejecting Jesus, Capernaum was to be "thrust down to Hell,"[16] while God's way of life draws man above, "that he may depart from Hell beneath."[17]

Drawing on this downward direction for Hell and the references in the Bible to its gates being in the deepest sea,[18] some believe that the abyss lies under the ocean. Pursuing the occult assertion that a lost civilization rests beneath the sea, they speculate that perhaps this is the abode of the damned, inhabited by demons and other fallen spirits. "Who should know better where demons live than those in the occult?" they ask.

If Hell lies hidden in the core of Earth, the theory continues, the shortest passage to it would be where the planet's crust is thinnest — within the 20,000 square mile area off Miami called the Bermuda Triangle and its parallel zone in the Philippine Sea known as the Devil's Triangle. "Could this account for the strange magnetic

disturbances and unexplained disappearances of
ships and airplanes?" they wonder.[19]

No one knows the location of Hell. But if the
rich man could come back today, this is what he
would say, "It is where peace can never come,
where joy is a stranger, music is alien, the sounds
of laughter are never heard, and where fellowship
is foreign. It is an inferno where each hapless soul
is incarcerated in the prison of his own memory,
where the deathly silence is broken only by the
wail of tortured souls as they remember the op-
portunities they so carelessly threw away. Hell is
beyond the sunshine of God's smile, the echo of
angels' songs, and the joy of children's laughter.
Hell is where loved ones never love again."

Is Hell Just?

Once a soul has fought its way into this pit,
there is no way out. Some ask, "How could a
loving and just God create such a place as this?
Where is the justice in that?"

Hell was not made for man! It was created as a
fitting retribution for Satan and the angels who
fell with him before the world began. The Bible
says:

> "Then shall he say also unto them on
> the left hand, Depart from me, ye
> cursed, into everlasting fire, prepared
> for the devil and his angels."[20]

People who go to Hell are intruders, sent there
only because they reject God's provision for re-
demption through Christ.

Beyond this, Hell is part of God's justice. Many times the world has seemed without justice. Wicked men seemingly prosper while the righteous perish. If judgment is not given beyond the grave, how can we justify the existence of dictators and war criminals who live out their lives in luxury with the blood of thousands on their hands? How would God's justice be served if John the Baptist and King Herod were to sit side by side along heavenly streams?

Consider what Heaven would be like for someone who had spent his life hating God. The brilliance of perfect love would be like a bolt of lightning, painfully searing the eyes in eternal torture. If you don't like church here, you will certainly hate Heaven. To spend eternity praising God would be excruciating for one in rebellion against Him. Feeling the infinitely probing eyes of God, exposing and condemning the sins of one not covered by the mercy of Christ, would be greater torment than the fires of the Pit. The infamous blasphemer Altamont declared on his deathbed, "Hell is a refuge if there I can hide from the eyes of God!"

Making us free beings, God scrupulously honors our liberty, even when it leads to destruction. Jesus diligently seeks to rescue us from damnation. But we must grasp for His lifeline. If we insist on continuing down the road to the abyss, He will sorrowfully let us go. The decision is ours.

The Downward Road

In racing down that road, people seem to ig-
nore the obstacles God has placed in their path to
make them turn around. Walking side by side on
this highway are the murderer and the "good"
man. The drunk staggers along, trying frantically
to keep pace with the one toiling under the
weight of hoarded riches.

When anyone falls, he must help himself or
perish; no brotherly love is shared on this
thoroughfare to Hell. The cloying smell of death
is everywhere, as are the agonies of loneliness,
cynicism and hatred. But the travelers set their
faces onward, refusing to heed the warnings of
their coming doom.

It's not easy to go to Hell, and the one who
ends up there will never be able to point an accus-
ing finger at God. He has given everyone abun-
dant opportunity to escape destruction. Any soul
who stubbornly persists in that direction leaves
behind the wreckage of every barrier God could
devise to halt the mad downward dash.

To reach Hell, one must ignore the greatest bar-
rier of all — the sacrifice of Jesus Christ on the
cross. Everyone who has heard the name of Jesus
is faced with a decision: What will you do with
Him? He lived in history, died and rose from the
grave. People are healed by His power. Lives are
transformed in an instant. The evidence is in-
escapable; only those who willfully ignore the
facts can continue to the lower world.

To reach Hell, one also must reject the
persistent, gentle tugging of the Holy Spirit to

surrender to God. The heart must become rock hard to block out the voice of the Spirit. The prayers of friends and relatives must be rejected, the words of truth in the Bible contradicted, and the living witness of God's people mocked in order to complete the downward journey. In the face of persistent divine efforts to turn this course, the one on Hell's highway must display singleminded stubbornness — and foolishness — to reach his destination.

Attempted Escape

Riding his exhausted horse into Tuscaloosa, Alabama, just as the sun was setting, an old man reined up in front of the only hotel and dragged himself to the registration desk.

The clerk stared in amazement as the man wearily asked for a single night's lodging.

"Don't you think you'll need more than one night's rest before continuing?" he ventured.

"Just sign me up for one night," the man replied feebly. "That's all I'll need. Tomorrow I'll be a corpse."

"You're tired and overwrought from your long journey," the clerk mumbled sympathetically. "I'll give you a comfortable bed. Tomorrow you'll feel better."

"Tomorrow I'll be a corpse," the man repeated. "When I am gone, sell the horse. It's yours. All I ask is that you bury me beside the old board sidewalk and place a headboard over my grave: 'You cannot run from the Spirit of God.' "

Shrugging his shoulders, the clerk readily gave his promise and forgot the matter. In the morning, he was startled by a scream from the maid. The stranger was dead in his bed. After examining the body, the coroner shook his head and frowned, "I can find no physical cause for his death. He died of mental agony."

Later the man's story came to light. He had attended a revival meeting where the Spirit of God had told him, "You must be born again!" With bitter rebellion in his soul, he declared, "I will not be born again!"

Again and again, the old gentleman heard the inward voice and each time refused. Determining to run from God, he filled his saddlebags with money and began to ride. Day and night he urged the beast on, trying to escape the haunting voice. But it was impossible.

At last in the lonely hotel room, he fought the final battle against the pleading Spirit of God. There he died in mental agony, without God and without hope.

For many years, the rough headboard stood on the street of Tuscaloosa, mutely testifying to man's persistence in running to Hell.

We decide our eternal destiny. God sends no one to the abyss who does not insist on it. Salvation is available to every soul who will accept Jesus, God's greatest gift to mankind. If one is eternally lost, it is because he wants to be. Thousands of excuses may be offered for shunning God, but not one reason.

In Hell one comes to the blood-chilling, terrifying realization that the final line has been crossed. God's last overture of mercy has been rejected, the gentle Holy Spirit spurned one time too many. Now, beyond the reach of grace and pardon, the soul is finally and utterly lost.

Hell is where the lifeline of Jesus' blood cannot reach, the one place from which God cannot answer prayer. It is the only pit from which God, with all His power, cannot extricate the soul, the one death with no hope for a resurrection to life. From this arid wasteland no seeds of life can grow.

Could anything be worse than this?

Difficult as it may seem, something is worse, magnifying Hell's torments many times over.

CHAPTER 3

A SECOND CHANCE IN DESTINY?

An instant after his car crashed headlong into the oak tree, Robert felt light as a feather. The flash of pain he had experienced was gone as he floated gently out of the body pinned in the tangled wreckage.

Hovering for a moment, he shot up at a dizzying speed toward a brilliant point of pure light sparkling in the nighttime sky. Almost immediately, the light diffused into the most incredibly beautiful sight he had ever seen. A city lay glistening beneath him as he approached, the sky almost transparent, bathing him in a pure golden light. The love he sensed felt like the purest moments of tenderness given to him by his mother.

"I must be going to Heaven," he thought. "I never believed in God or life after death, but it must really be true!"

Descending gently into the outskirts of the celestial city, Robert smiled as he scanned the clusters of beautiful flowers, gently winding roads, and trees bearing fragrant fruit beyond imagination. In the distance he could see happy people walking together, their garments shimmering in the exquisite rainbow light.

Suddenly, Robert found himself facing a radiant being, whose vibrant luminosity dazzled his eyes. Intense waves of light and love rolled over him, one after another, infusing such complete peace and joy that he could hardly stand.

"Is this Heaven?" he asked the being.

"You are standing on the outskirts of the heavenly city," the glowing one replied.

Tears filled Robert's eyes as he gazed at the splendors in the distance. "All I've ever dreamed of, all I looked for in life is right here," he marveled. "I could not have imagined a place more beautiful!"

The next words brought him up short. "You cannot enter the city," the being of light said calmly. "Only those who belong to Me can become citizens here. The weight of evil in your life would make it too painful for you to stay. You will have to spend eternity in Hell."

Robert's joy shaded suddenly into fear as he realized with whom he was speaking. Here was the Christ he had rejected and ignored, casually cursing Him so many times in everyday conversation.

Instantly, the intense radiation of love flickered out, replaced by a powerful probe of pure energy. Having just felt so wonderfully loved, Robert now experienced an equally intense feeling of guilt and shame. Every evil thought, every wrong action that had been part of his life simultaneously filled his consciousness. All of the hate, lust and greed from years on Earth burst into his awareness in a single, overwhelming flash.

Robert staggered under the load. The vile self-loathing he experienced was beyond imagination. "How could I have been so evil?" he wondered incredulously. "God gave me so many opportunities to change, and I threw them all away. I have no one to blame but myself!"

"As you chose to reject God on Earth," Jesus continued, "so your decision will be honored in eternity. However, it is still possible to change. Your time has not yet come to enter the afterworld. Go back now, and act on what you have learned."

With a tremendous tug, Robert was pulled back into the pain-filled body lying in the car wreck. Returning to consciousness, he knew for certain that something was worse than Hell.

All of us will face God in judgment, bringing our meager accomplishments before His infinite justice. Sensing His love, seeing the beauties of the celestial city, then being flung into eternal damnation would be worse than Hell itself. Forever lamenting the tranquil beauties that were exchanged for eternal torment, the underworld resident will find his anguish multiplied manyfold.

One need not travel outside the body to realize the splendors of Heaven. How many of those attending church on Sunday morning have heard the gospel, yet ignored its message? Surely the memory of that rejection will be worse than the endless tortures of the Pit.

Unlike Robert, the average person is not given a second chance. At the moment of death it is too late to change; the course set on Earth continues

forever. Hell is not a correctional institution from
which the prisoner is released once a term is
served. It is forever; there the door of mercy is
closed.

Great Rewards — Great Punishments

How could decisions made in this life count for
eternity? A sincere look into the Bible reveals
they do. If we could comprehend all the ways of
God, compressing Him within the paltry limits of
human rationality, He would be no wiser, no
greater than we. Comparing the wisdom of God
with that of man is like correlating the majestic
art of Michelangelo to the meaningless daubs of a
child on a piece of scrap paper.

In Proverbs we read:
> "The Lord by wisdom hath founded
> the earth; by understanding hath He
> established the heavens."[1]

The Apostle Paul wrote:
> "O the depths of the riches both of
> the wisdom and knowledge of God!
> How unsearchable are His judgments,
> and His ways past finding out!
>
> The foolishness of God is wiser than
> men; and the weakness of God is
> stronger than men."[2]

God is under no obligation to be understood
by man, nor is it on this basis that He deals with
us. Motivated by pure love, He has provided per-
fect salvation, atoning for sin by a complete

sacrifice and furnishing an externally flawless place for all those who receive His salvation. He does not ask nor expect us to understand all this. He asks us to accept it!

I cannot understand all that God does, but I know He acts with reason. He has a purpose for Heaven and a just rationale for Hell.

It Shall Never End

The knowledge that no matter how long one has been there it is only the beginning of a dreadful eternal existence — that understanding adds immeasurably to Hell's afflictions.

The Bible says:

> "The smoke of their torment ascendeth up forever and ever: and they have no rest day nor night . . ."[3]

Hell is described as "everlasting fire;" its punishment is eternal,[4] with a "fire that never shall be quenched."[5] Make no mistake about it: the abyss is forever. The day will never come when the living dead will say, "We've come halfway through," for after ten million times ten million years have rolled over the lake of fire, eternity will have just begun.

How long is forever? Picture a tiny sparrow transplanting the Earth, one grain at a time, to a star system billions of miles away. If it took a million years for each round trip, eternity would have just started; the suffering of the lost would be just beginning. Yet something worse than the

knowledge of endless punishment is in store for
the residents of the infernal abyss.

No One Alone

Not one of us goes through life by ourselves.
We either add or take something away from the
lives of others. A cynic inevitably will infect
others with his bitterness. A skeptic will fill
others with unbelief. *There is something worse
than going to hell. It is the knowledge that you
don't go alone.*

Imagine your anguish at knowing you had led
your own loved ones to the lower world. Visual-
ize those innocent faces that trusted your leader-
ship now distorted by the agonies of damnation:
a son who imitated the false example of manhood
you presented; a daughter who saw in you a way
of life deceptively leading to destruction. Now,
remember the times on Earth when little faces
beamed with trust that Dad and Mom were right.

I assure you that the torment of Hell itself is
far less than the never ending agony of seeing
young people there because they followed you.
Husband, looking down Hell's corridors at your
wife throughout eternity is worse than Hell.
Think now of the unending torment, "I led my
loved one here."

Perhaps now you can understand the misery of
the rich man in Hades as he sought relief from the
agonies he felt, crying out for his loved ones who
would surely join him there. He loved his five

brothers still on Earth and would have done anything to save them, but he was powerless. Envision the excruciating agony of knowing he had influenced them wrongly, and everlasting fire was their destiny. That eternal weight of guilt was more oppressive than all the gruesome tortures of the Pit.

Influence of Religious Tradition

What will be the guilt of religious leaders who deny the existence of Hell, telling their followers that God will overlook sin?

There was a well known minister in a large conservative denomination for fifty-two years before he met Jesus personally. During those decades, this man denied the existence of Heaven and Hell, the virgin birth of Jesus and other fundamental Christian doctrines. His ministry bore the fruit of his disbelief: To his knowledge, not a single person came to Jesus during the whole period, according to his testimony.

What an influence this popular pastor could have had during that half-century. How many could have escaped the fiery consequences of his work had he not led them into misleading religious experiences.

At age seventy, this man accepted Jesus as his Savior and was born again. Since then, it has been a different story, for thousands have been brought to Christ through his influence. How terrible Hell would have been for this influential minister, but think of how joyous Heaven will be as he joins those he led to Christ.

Some congregations are so cold and self-centered they look askance at anyone seeking an exit from the road to damnation. Their hostile glances tell him, "We don't want your kind here."

On one occasion I was invited by a church of a major denomination to participate in a series of studies on the Book of Revelation. After I presented the truths of the second coming of Christ and future events taught in the book, the host pastor began to undermine what I had said.

"Of course, we no longer accept the view presented today by Jerry," he smiled at the audience. "Through years of study, we have developed a better understanding of these teachings."

The minister then held up a denominational study book for all to see. "Through our study, we have developed this guide; we follow this rather than just the Bible, as Jerry does. Today, we have grown beyond this teaching of the return of Christ and the outdated concepts of Heaven and Hell."

Others teach that the way to Heaven is long and difficult, demanding such determined effort and so many good deeds that few can make it.

While sitting in a barber shop one day awaiting my turn for a haircut, I became acquainted with a member of a prominent local church. I was startled by the turn of our conversation.

"If you're not baptized in our church," he said firmly, "You're not in the body of Christ."

"You mean to tell me I'm not a Christian because I'm not baptized in <u>your</u> church and haven't done what your church requires?" I frowned, trying to camouflage my dismay.

"That's right!"

On another occasion, I was standing in a church in Honolulu, Hawaii, asking the minister for the use of his building for some special services. Our conversation turned to the requirements for going to Heaven. Keeping the letter of the law, abstaining from certain foods and strict observance of Saturday as a day of worship were important issues to the clergyman.

I was shocked by his assertion: Unless one subscribes to all that church's teachings, he will not go to Heaven.

Other churches set such strict requirements of dress and conduct that people are driven sorrowfully away. My own father in his early ministry was in a denomination where it was considered sinful to wear jewelry. Those refusing to remove even a wedding band were not allowed to join the church. Although troubled by these rules, he taught them because they were required by his superiors. As Dad's ministry matured, he realized such strict codes were not necessary to salvation. Eventually, he left that organization and forsook the man-made laws. Just before he died, my father asked me tearfully, "Do you think God will hold me accountable for those who were turned away?"

My answer was, "Dad, God forgives, and in the joy of Heaven, no memory will torment."

Christians Have Influence

One need not be a religious leader to drive peo-
ple away from God. How many times has some-
one said, "Those Christians are a bunch of
hypocrites. I knew a guy who thought he was
holy, but here's what he was really like . . . ."?
Worst of all, the story is sometimes true!

Those outside the church often seem to know
how a believer should act and react better than
the Christian does. If you claim to be a child of
God, you will be watched closely. If your life
meets the standard, it will have tremendous posi-
tive effect. If not, remember that also is an in-
fluence — away from God.

How many are turned away from God by a
Christian who doesn't pay his bills or by a church
member whose morals are questionable? Tragi-
cally, many residents of the abyss can say of a
"Christian," "He led me here."

When I was pastoring in Sacramento several
years ago, a nationally famous evangelist came to
town. His ministry contained all the worst ele-
ments of a pseudo-evangelistic operation: fabri-
cated miracles, gimmicks and razzle-dazzle,
money-grabbing methods.

Refusing to support this man in our city, I
found myself the object of his strongest attacks.
"If you do not support the meetings," he warned
me, "I will see your church put out of business
and you run out of town!"

After a period of intense loneliness as others
deserted me, I was gloriously vindicated when the

people began to see the true motive of this man.
God blessed our ministry many times over. This
man moves to new areas each time he is exposed,
and I cannot help but wonder how many people
are permanently turned away from Christ because
of his ethics.[6]

Sowing Eternal Seeds

One of the worst influences a Christian can
have is none at all. He can work with and live side
by side with one who is sliding headlong into
destruction, doing nothing to deter him from his
diabolical destiny. To this kind of person,
Christianity is merely a Sunday morning ad-
venture. He gives little or nothing to the church
and makes no effort to witness about the faith
that feebly smolders within. Surely, this must
multiply the torment of the person in Hell, think-
ing of all the opportunities that a Christian friend
had to alter his fate.

We cannot escape the fact that we sow eternal
seeds every day. Some have brought forth an
abundant crop of eternal righteousness; others
have reaped a harvest of horror. Like a creeping
destruction, the seeds of sin drag millions of souls
down into the Pit. Children follow their parents,
wives their husbands, and husbands their wives to
the regions of the damned.

For those in Hell, it is too late to repent. They
are left with the memory of their own failure and
perhaps the bitter knowledge that a Christian al-
lowed them to go there.

No wonder the rich man in Hades, after realizing his eternity was sealed, cried in anguish, "Send someone to warn my five brothers not to follow me to this place." The same cry is being echoed this very moment as millions scream in agony, knowing someone on Earth is going to enter the torment of Hell because of their influence during life.

But for the living, change is possible as long as breath remains. No one need go to Hell.

CHAPTER 4

UNDER THE INFLUENCE OF WHOM?

Singing in the midst of a midnight earthquake, Paul and Silas hurried to stop the frightened Philippian jailer from killing himself for fear his prisoners had escaped.

"We're all here!" Paul called to him.

Astonished that these amazing apostles actually lived what they preached, the jailer fell to his knees.

"What must I do to be saved?" he stammered.

"Believe on the Lord Jesus and you will be saved, together with your household," Paul answered. Within the hour, the whole family had become Christians and were baptized.[1]

All of us have a father or a mother, brother or sister, nephew or cousin we would dearly like to see brought into God's kingdom. How can we bring them with us into the life beyond?

Many view this passage as a guarantee of their loved ones' salvation, and I would be the last to dash their hopes. But let's be honest: This story is not a promise that the entire family will be saved because one member is a Christian. It is an account of a real incident that we can take example

from. The jailer believed in Jesus and was re-
deemed. In the same way, his household believed
in Jesus (after Paul and Silas had told them the
gospel), and they also were saved. Although it is
not a guarantee, it is certainly a wonderful bibli-
cal truth that we can claim.

God never goes against our free will. If you are
praying for the salvation of your loved ones and
they resist the drawing power of the Holy Spirit,
God will not force them to accept Christ. This
would make men puppets, robots, not free moral
agents as the Bible teaches. Salvation is an indi-
vidual experience, requiring each person to accept
or reject. Yet God has faithfully promised that
nothing is impossible with Him. He can make a
way where there seems to be no way. God will
answer the prayer of faith.

Our hopes of their coming to the Lord is by
our constant prayer and godly influence. Prayer
moves God to extraordinary measures in bringing
our loved ones to Him. Giving them multiplied
opportunities, He often performs miracles to
show them the reality of Jesus Christ, just as He
did Saul on the road to Damascus, transforming
him into Paul the Apostle.[2] Similarly, living a
consistent Christian life based on biblical princi-
ples will do more to influence others toward God
than all the preaching in the world. Backed by
these forces, we are in His will to claim by faith
the salvation of our family and cling to that
blessed hope despite all outward circumstances.

No one is so wicked and vile that God is unable
to reach him. It doesn't matter how deep the evil,

how sick the soul. Never give up, even if you are standing by someone's deathbed, watching him gasp for his last breath. God can save until the moment the threshold of eternity is crossed.

Our fight is not against flesh and blood, but against the mighty forces of Satan and the evil princes of the spirit world.[3] The only way to release our loved ones from the chains of these demonic powers is constant prayer, and with fasting if the Lord leads. We are the ones who make the difference in the spiritual warfare.

On their own, non-Christians cannot make the change; only the Spirit of God can lead them. Deluded and blind, they are bound by an enemy they are not even aware of. Talk to them about church, and they mutter, "Huh! Who needs it?" Discuss the Bible, and they wrinkle their noses, "How boring!"

But this imprisonment can be broken through intercessory prayer. Eventually, the ice will begin to melt, and little by little they will turn toward God. Believe, and soon you'll be rejoicing with them as they enter God's kingdom. We can take courage in this promise from the Bible: "What things soever ye desire, when ye pray, believe that ye receive them, and ye shall have them."[4]

The triumph of Dr. and Mrs. Harvey Lifsey is testimony to the power of this verse and other promises in the Bible. Here's how they battled for a rebellious daughter and won:

> "Our precious daughter was never really part of our family. From a child, she seemed distant and withdrawn.

Never once did she say, "I'm sorry;"
no matter how we disciplined her, she
responded with rebellion.

This contrary spirit developed in seri-
ous proportions during junior high,
then exploded while she was in high
school. We discovered that our daugh-
ter was on drugs, involved with im-
morality, liquor and crime. Finally,
when nothing we could do would help,
we realized our daughter was under a
powerful demonic deception and was
being dominated by evil powers. At this
point, God showed us that our daugh-
ter could be set free only as we took
our authority in Jesus Christ.

God quickened our hearts to the
promise in Matthew 18:18,19, that
"Whatsoever ye shall bind on earth
shall be bound in heaven: and whatso-
ever ye shall loose on earth shall be
loosed in heaven . . . If two of you shall
agree on earth as touching any thing
that they shall ask, it shall be done for
them of my Father which is in heaven."

As we took hold of these promises,
my wife and I agreed in prayer, binding
the powers of darkness over our daugh-
ter and releasing her mind to the truth
of Jesus Christ. We prayed that the
Spirit of God would bring His convict-
ing power upon her life and that He
would awaken her spiritual sensitivity.

Instead of the instant change we expected, she grew worse. And worse. Refusing to accept this response, we began in faith to praise God for His promises and to think, talk and pray according to the promises of God.

Within two weeks, my wife led our daughter to the Lord. Completely transformed, she threw away her rock music, tore up her tapes, and destroyed all her narcotics. It was the most glorious change that we have ever seen. Now she is in college preparing to serve the Lord as a physical education director. Christ has broken the power of demonic forces and sin over her life and has set her free.

It hasn't been victory without setback, however. She slipped back into discouragement a couple of times, but as we interceded and claimed God's promises, we watched our daughter grow into a consistent walk with Jesus."

While you are praying for your loved ones, strive to present a godly example of Jesus. Always ask, "What would Jesus do?" Then do likewise. Preaching at family members probably will drive them away from God; lovingly demonstrating what Christ can do in your life will draw them like a magnet. True Christianity is one of the world's best-kept secrets. Let people see a real Christian, and few can resist his beauty.

A Wife's Influence

Mickie Butler's husband John came from a good religious background, but he wanted nothing to do with God. She often nagged him about attending church, but his response was a stubborn "No."

One evening as Mickie contemplated visiting another church, John suggested, "We've seen that Jerry Barnard on television, why don't you go to his church?"

"That's a neat idea, John," she beamed, snuggling closer to him on the couch. "Wouldja like to come with me?"

"Mickie! We've been through all this a million times!" John broke away and stormed toward the kitchen. "How many times must I say no before you finally get the message?" He paused at the doorway and jabbed his index finger in her direction. "Now lay off!"

"Well! It wouldn't hurt you to go just once!" she spat. "I'm always alone."

The following night her sleep was filled with a dream in which she and John attended our church together. Waking up, Mickie claimed the dream as a promise from God.

As the week continued, she prayed impatiently for her husband. Her desperation rising because nothing had yet happened, she cried, "Lord, if you love me, you'll let the pastor say my name Sunday as a sign my prayers are getting through!" Instantly ashamed, she checked the thought.

"That's ridiculous, Lord. I know better than that. Please forgive me. I don't need a sign."

The next Sunday one of the pastors of Christian Faith Centre felt led during the service to call Mickie out, not knowing of her prayer. "Mickie Butler," he said, "raise your hand." Waving excitedly, she knew God was answering her prayer. "Lord, I know you're there," she cried. "Thank you for the answer."

Mother's Day was coming, and John asked her what she wanted for the occasion.

"I'd like for you to go to church with me," she replied apprehensively. "Now . . . before you say no, remember you asked. Besides, Mother's Day is special." In her voice was all the charm she could muster.

John glared at her for a moment, then softened. "Aw, all right. But only this once." Mickie planted a kiss on his cheek and smiled to herself, "Sure, dear."

When the day arrived, he dragged himself out of bed just before it was time to leave and accompanied her to church. Determined not to listen or blink an eye, he glared stone-faced at every person around him during the service.

Mickie was disturbed. "How can he receive anything with that attitude?" she muttered.

One of their friends was to be baptized that evening, and somehow she persuaded him to go again. Sitting beside John, so rigid in the midst of God's presence, Mickie began to cry. "I just can't stand it, Lord," she prayed quietly. She was sure he would melt down and join in the worship, but he stubbornly refused.

After the service, the friend who had been bap-
tized walked up to Mickie. "Don't worry about
it," he smiled reassuringly. "I just know John
asked Jesus into his life, though only in his mind.
He'll come around."

"Did he tell you something he didn't tell me?"
her eyes reflected confusion.

"No, I just know it somehow. Don't worry."

The next Sunday, Mickie again persuaded John
to attend church. "You'll just watch it on TV
anyway, so you might as well go!" By now, he
was a little more open. Thumbing through a song
book, he recalled how he and his sisters had trav-
eled, singing gospel songs as children. Yet he had
never been told how to find Jesus personally and,
because of an environment of hypocrisy, had
been driven from God.

Turning to the song, Amazing Grace, John rec-
ognized his favorite hymn. Mickie pointed to the
words, "how sweet the sound that saved a wretch
like me." and said, "Read those words. They're
for you."

John mumbled, "If God wants me, He'll have
to throw my hands up in the air, and I won't have
anything to say about it."

"Grab him, Lord," Mickie prayed. "He wants
it."

At the end of the service, I asked those who
wanted to receive Christ to come forward. In
answer to Mickie's prayer, John walked down the
aisle with her. Kneeling at the altar, he said, "I
have wanted to know Jesus all my life, but I
don't."

Praying for Jesus to take charge of his life, suddenly his arms shot up into the air, and John turned to his wife with a radiant smile. "I've found Him," he beamed. "Now we can be open with each other. I don't have to hide anymore!"

Looking back on her attempts to force John to the Lord, Mickie regrets being so insistent. "I think I probably did more harm than good when it came to his salvation," she recalls. "If I had been more submissive and less boastful of my feelings, he probably would have come to Jesus a lot sooner. He was going to come when he was ready and not a second before. God saved him in spite of me."

The Bible commands:

> "Wives, submit yourselves unto your own husbands, as unto the Lord. For the husband is the head of the wife, even as Christ is the head of the church . . . Therefore as the church is subject unto Christ, so let the wives be to their own husbands in every thing . . . (Let) the wife see that she reverence her husband."[5]

With all the misguided and unbiblical ideas about "liberation" today, it is often difficult for a wife to find her proper role. But I believe she can love her husband right into the kingdom of God if she will reverence and obey him and learn to be loving and kind. Forgiveness is a principle that always works. Forgiving their wrongs and shortcomings makes it easier to let Jesus love them through you. A husband will never be convinced

by threats or nagging. Only by living a biblical
relationship with him as far as possible, and pray-
ing constantly, will a wife draw her husband to
Jesus.

A Husband's Influence

Sometimes a Christian husband will have as
much difficulty bringing an unsaved wife to God.
His responsibility, for a start, is to practice the
command given in Ephesians 5:25.

> "Husbands, love your wives, even as
> Christ also loved the church, and gave
> himself for it."

God intends husbands to be the head of the
family, taking the lead first in giving love. In-
fluenced by movies and novels, men and women
often view love through a romantic haze as some-
thing one may feel today but not tomorrow.
While emotion has a beautiful place in love, its
essence is commitment to the other person. When
a man takes the marriage vows, he promises God
to give his wife the best he has. That's love in
action.

If a Christian husband lives according to bibli-
cal principles, he is in an excellent position to
lead his wife to Jesus. Wives are looking for loving
leadership, not demanding dominance. Jesus is
Head of the church, but His leadership is exer-
cised in love and patience.

Another aspect of headship in the family is to
break loose from the control of parents. The

Bible says:

> "For this cause shall a man leave his
> father and mother, and shall be joined
> unto his wife, and they two shall be
> one flesh."[6]

At the marriage altar, parents were left behind
and a totally new union was formed. Parents are
not deserted nor their love rejected, but the rela-
tionship is suddenly different. A husband should
make his wife the most important person on
Earth. Parents on neither side of the new family
should be allowed to run the household.

The Christian husband must be the priest of his
family. Study the examples of Abraham, Noah,
Isaac and Jacob in light of New Testament teach-
ings. Godly priesthood involves four responsibili-
ties:

First, <u>a priest is called of God.</u> Whether or not
his wife is a Christian, the husband has a responsi-
bility given by God. Fill the calling; don't com-
promise. Evangelists minister to thousands, but
each husband can minister directly to his own
family.

Second, <u>a priest is separated unto God</u>. Called
to holiness, Christian husbands must live apart
from evil. Decisions for the family, and especially
the children's upbringing, should be made prayer-
fully and according to biblical principles. You are
responsible before God for the direction your
family takes.

Third, <u>a priest directs spiritual activities in the
family</u>. You are God's representative, assuming
spiritual leadership. Take the initiative and allow

your wife the opportunity to share. Good leadership is not demonstrated in harshness or demanding tones but by godly example and loving teaching.

Fourth, a <u>priest intercedes for others.</u> The Christian husband especially must pray constantly for his wife, never giving up on behalf of her salvation. If necessary, you must wrestle with the powers of Satan until their hold is broken.

The Christian husband cannot force his wife to her knees. Only God can perform this miracle. A wise husband will pray in faith for Holy Spirit intervention, then make room for it to happen.

The Influence of Parents

Charlotte Reid had attended church most of her life and thought she had enough faith to trust God for the care of her family. Yet when her husband left after twenty years of marriage, Charlotte's world collapsed.

"At least I have my children," she mused.

But one after another, her dreams fell apart. One girl broke up with her boyfriend in law school, another became involved with drugs; her son dropped out of school, and her married daughter left her husband, eventually ending up in a mental hospital.

"Oh, God, what's happening?" Charlotte cried, begging the Lord to help her manage the situation. One day during a prayer group meeting in our church, Assistant Pastor Hal Adams asked, "Charlotte, aren't you sick of worrying?"

"Yes! I'm tired of it," she sighed.

"If you don't stop carrying all these problems on your back, they'll destroy you," he warned.

No one had ever talked to her that way, but in her spirit she knew it was from the Lord.

"What should I do?" she wept. "I've prayed and prayed. I've done everything, but things don't seem to change."

"Release your children to God, Charlotte. Let Him handle even your future," he counseled.

"I've never been a meddling mother," she protested.

"I'm sure you haven't, Charlotte. But God loves your children more than you do. Don't you think He can do a better job of taking care of them – if you let Him?"

Releasing the children to the Lord and trusting Him, Charlotte saw God work miracles. The married daughter was reunited with her husband as he lovingly brought her out of the hospital. Her son found a good job and soon received two promotions. Another daughter is happily married, and the third has broken off an unhealthy relationship and is turning more and more to God.

"I haven't been this happy in years," Charlotte beams. "I thank God for loving people who took me to church and Bible study, who prayed with me when my heart was broken and taught me to release my children to God."

Besides prayer, our children need leadership as they grow. The Book of Proverbs says:

Train up a child in the way he should
go: and when he is old, he will not

depart from it.

"Withhold not correction from the child: for if thou beatest him with the rod, he shall not die . . . (but) his soul (shall be delivered) from hell."[7]

A recent survey of American families with children under the age of thirteen indicated that children had the same needs regardless of income level, education or parental philosophy:

1. A mother at home who would cook and keep the house;
2. A father as the principal wage earner who would spend time with them;
3. Times of recreation as a family;
4. They did not object to spankings and
5. Wanted the parents to remain together at all costs.

Children need security, love and leadership. They want parents who will tell them how far to go and no further. They're hungry for love, the warm touch of a father and mother, and spiritual guidance. Because many roads sparkle with the lights of attraction, we must not leave our children to find God on their own.

Parents, don't be afraid to keep your children away from bad influences. It is your responsibility to make decisions that are best for your child. Train them in good health habits. Limit television viewing. Meet and help choose their friends. Bring them to church. Discipline them in love. Pray with them and share the Bible. Set a godly example. Keep your sons and daughters before God in prayer every day; raise them in a Christian atmosphere, then trust God to do the rest. As a result, you have every promise that they will turn to Jesus.

Influence of Children

My wife Sandi and I prayed long hours for her parents' salvation. They had attended church for about a year when she was born, but soon were driven out by rigid and false doctrine. Church leaders made it difficult to be saved. Their form of Christianity was based on experience and rigid rules rather than the Bible.

Years later in another city, one of Sandi's three older brothers fell in love with a Christian girl and began attending church with her. One evening, the couple invited Sandi's parents to accompany them, and surprisingly, they went. Times were difficult, and they were having a few marital problems. Perhaps going back to church would help.

The Holy Spirit was moving over the Bible-centered congregation, and everything seemed right for her parents to come to God.

Sandi relates what happened:

> Mom and Dad sat in the back of the church, each holding a baby and trying to listen as the minister preached. Daddy knew the strain of providing for a large family, and Mother was feeling the pressures of many burdens.

Listening to a message of God's love,
both of them felt hope rising in their
hearts. Meanwhile, the babies were get-
ting restless.

Just in front of them sat one of the
"pillars" of the church and his wife.
They turned and stared coldly at these
noisy strangers. Mom and Dad were dis-
tracted but tried to listen to the evan-
gelist. Soon the head usher came by,
fresh from counting the offering, and
he also returned my father's smile with
a cold glare.

As the baby she held whimpered,
Mother began to gather up the child's
things to take him to the nursery. Im-
patiently, the usher and the woman in
front of them acted without wisdom.
"Will you please take the children
out?" they spat. Deeply hurt, the
whole family stood up and left the ser-
vice, not understanding the actions of
these church members. The speaker just
watched in helplessness. He had felt
God reaching this couple, and now they
were being driven out into the night.
Would they ever be back?

Later when nine-year-old Sandi asked Jesus
into her heart, she was discouraged from return-
ing to church because of the experience her par-
ents had encountered.

"You're too young to be accountable for sin,"
her mother told her, having been taught that

children are not responsible until twelve years of age. "Let Daddy and I carry that responsibility."

That night Sandi knelt by her bed and prayed, "Dear Jesus, it doesn't seem fair that I must wait 'till I'm twelve. But when I get to be a big girl, then I will serve you."

God remembered that promise and continued to deal with her heart. One night in her teenage years, Sandi dreamed she went to Hell, and there among the screaming victims were her parents. She reached out to help them but could not. Carrying the impression of that dream for a long time, she was concerned that her loved ones may be eternally lost.

But what could she do?

The memory of that doomed hopelessness haunted her. She didn't know where to turn for help. Her brothers were married. Her father worked long hours. Her mother was often sick and worried with raising a family. Then God sent a Christian girl, Darlene Schuman, to become Sandi's friend. Because of Darlene's influence, Sandi was finally persuaded to attend church with her.

"That evening as the altar call was being given, a beautiful, elegant lady came back to me," Sandi recalls. "She put her arms around me and said, 'Jesus loves you. Wouldn't you like to invite Him into your heart?' " These were words she had longed to hear.

With tears filling her eyes, Sandi knelt at the altar and was truly born again. Walking home from church that night, she knew she was a different person. The moonlight was much brighter, her

senses more alert. "This time no one can talk me
out of it," she determined.

At that point she began a two-year prayer bat-
tle for her parents' salvation. Although her
mother tried to discourage her from too much
church attendance, Sandi's love and devotion to
Jesus remained firm.

Determined her parents would receive Jesus be-
fore our wedding date, we made a prayer pact,
claiming the Bible verse, "If two of you shall
agree on earth as touching any thing that they
shall ask, it shall be done . . . ."[8] We set aside
every Monday for prayer and fasting on their be-
half.

We were away at Bible college then, and during
the time we prayed, we received letters from
Sandi's mother telling of her father's "heart at-
tacks." The doctor said his heart was fine, but
every time he went on a weekend drinking binge,
his chest pains returned. "Uncle Jesse" was a
"good ole boy" to his fellow workers at the Buick
factory, and drinking, storytelling and gambling
were part of the image he maintained. As the at-
tacks continued, fear gripped his heart. He
couldn't understand what was wrong with him,
but we knew.

During school holidays, we returned home. I
was scheduled to preach a two-week meeting in
my father's church. Our prayers intensified daily.

Fresh from Bible school studies, I was ready to
preach the great crusade of the century, already
envisioning the jeweled crowns we would receive
for the salvation of Sandi's family. But it didn't
happen the first week!

On Sunday morning — six short days before the crusade was to close — I arrived at Sandi's house to pick her up for church. Unknown to us, her mother was watching out the bedroom window as we drove happily away. So moved by our joy, she fell to her knees by the bed and tearfully gave her heart to Jesus.

When Sandi came home that early afternoon, her father was in the kitchen beginning his plans for the day.

"C'mon, go with me to the party," he begged.

"No, Jesse," his wife replied. "I'm not going with you anymore. I've changed my way of living."

"Well," he muttered, "If the Lord will let me live until I get sober, I'll get saved, too!"

Rushing to the phone, Sandi called me with the news, and we rejoiced together for her mother's salvation. We prayed that her father would attend our next service, though he had been drinking when he made his promise. God had a better plan than ours. Sandi continues the story:

> "On Tuesday at the factory, Dad found himself singing a hymn he'd heard me sing around the house. As he thought about the words, the old feelings of long ago rushed into his heart, and he began to cry while working at his machine.

> Being the big joker and gambler, he felt he couldn't let anyone see him cry, so he tried wiping the tears from his eyes. They wouldn't stop.

Across the factory aisle from him was a pastor who worked there to supplement his income. Unknown to any of us, he also had been praying for Daddy and talking to him about the Lord.

Noticing Daddy crying and singing, he walked over and threw his arm around him. "Jesse," he said gently, "Now's the time to accept Christ." Right there in the grease and sawdust, the two men knelt in front of all his buddies and prayed for Dad's salvation. Jesus came into his life in answer to prayer."

He came to the church where I was speaking that night, already a child of God. Once again God showed that He is in charge and that He is faithful to answer our prayers. In time, the whole family came to the Lord. Two of Sandi's brothers eventually entered the ministry.

Jesse's influence has turned hundreds to God. Beginning in the factory where he worked, he received permission to hold a Bible study and prayer time during the lunch hour. More than ninety men, including most of his friends, met Jesus in those factory meetings, and two of them became missionaries. In the years following, many others have come to Christ through his witness. Though nearly eighty years old, Sandi's father still participates in visitation projects for his church.

More than prayer is needed to influence parents for Christ, however. God's Word teaches us to obey them. A child may not always understand the decisions and directives of his mother and father, but obedience is the godly response. Presenting a Christlike example by living in obedience is one of the best ways to lead them into Heaven.

Children seeking the salvation of their parents need to hold fast to the Word of God, pray faithfully and live the life of Christ in the family.

Influence on Friends

People are desperately seeking models. As traditional roles disappear, confused individuals grope for someone to admire and follow. Many emulate celebrities, mirroring their sordid love affairs in search for pleasure. Others pursue the values of successful businessmen, perhaps sacrificing honesty in exchange for a few extra dollars.

How many follow you? Are they attracted by your sense of purpose, quiet joy, Christian ethics and closeness to God? The greatest tribute amid Heaven's accolades will be when people point to you in the heart of God's capital city and say, "You led me here!"

When the Holy Spirit fills us with compassion, we must do something about it. Has the Lord placed a burden on your heart for the salvation of a friend, business associate, neighbor, or even a stranger? Trust Him to fulfill that longing, and pray for the persons's salvation. Fast, if God directs. Hang on to that divine hope, and pray until it is accomplished.

When God directs you to take action, do it immediately. I met Father Robert Hanlon in 1975 during a cruise seminar aboard the M.S. Starward in the Caribbean. He was a chaplain for the ship, and some of our group invited him to hear me teach one afternoon.

Sitting with him at a table after my lecture, I began to share my joy in Christ. I could sense his hunger for this reality.

"Will you pray with me?" he finally asked.

"Yes . . . of course," I replied cautiously.

Taking him by the hand, I bowed my head. "Lord, may this man know the reality and true love of Jesus Christ." Just a simple prayer, but one with life-changing results. Sometime later, he recounted what God began in his life that day. Here are excerpts from his letters:

> "You were the instrument for grace for me. The experience on the ship was momentous. You said to me that day that July first would be memorable for me, and it was.
>
> When you prayed for me, it was an emotional experience that affected me deeply and permanently. I was inundated by the Spirit.
>
> I remember praying and crying all through the following evening, simply repeating the name "Jesus" and nothing more. I became certain that I was saved.
>
> I am now reading Scripture with more interest and fruit. I am spending

longer time at prayer. I have a new
spontaneity."
Only God knows the time when someone is
ready to surrender to Jesus as Lord of his life, as
in the case of Father Hanlon. Jumping ahead of
the Lord may drive one to stubbornness. Waiting
too long may allow a heart to become unbreak-
ably hardened.

The Greatest Witness

The greatest witness we can have is our love.
"See how they love one another" was the in-
credulous whisper among the first century citi-
zens who gazed in fascinated wonder at this new
breed of men and women called Christians.

The love shown in our church to Charlotte
Reid kept her coming back until she developed a
living faith in Jesus. In turn Charlotte's unfailing
love for her wayward children brought them to
God. How different the story of Sandi's parents
might have been if they had found love in the
church instead of icy stares!

Christian love can be demonstrated by support-
ing your home church as well as worthy Christian
outreach ministries. Not all of us can reach the
multitudes for Christ, feed the hungry or clothe
the needy. Few are called to spread the gospel
beyond the seas or across our borders. But all of
us can share our wealth for God's work.

Picture the unknown faces awaiting us in
Heaven because of our generous contributions to

ministries on Earth. Each one we meet there in
whose salvation we played even a small part will
add that much more to the joys of Paradise.

Time and Talents

Beyond finances, we all have talents to help
bring others into the kingdom. Some can sing;
others are able to attract many admiring friends.
Still others have only a smile to give. Whatever
our ability, we can use it in the service of Christ.

Once pastoring a large church in Indiana and
active in a Bible institute, Christian high school,
and radio and television ministries, Paul and
Jenny Billheimer were forced to retire because of
failing health.

In sorrow and disappointment, the couple set-
tled into a little cabin deep in the Georgia woods.
There Reverend Billheimer, past seventy, sat with
his wife waiting to die. Lives over, visions in
shambles, they had already reserved a burial plot
in a nearby cemetery.

Yet in the depths of their despair, a desire grew
in Paul's heart to share just one more message
with a lost world. He decided to write a book.
For many long months, the couple struggled to
produce the manuscript, interrupted by cancer,
physical exhaustion and severe heart attacks.
Finally, Destined for the Throne was completed
and published. Nearly a quarter million books
have been sold. Life took on a new beginning for
the Billheimers, and this is how it came about:

Christian Faith Centre was holding its third annual Conference on the Holy Spirit, and I knew we should have the Billheimers present. We had never met, and I didn't know how to reach them. We certainly had no idea of the problems they had experienced. I instructed one of my assistant pastors, Gil Jones, to invite Reverend Billheimer to our conference. When Gil finally reached him, he stammered, "You don't know what you're asking. I am eighty years old."

"Congratulations!" Gil responded. "Now, about the conference. May we count on you to teach?"

As the conversation continued, Reverend Billheimer realized this was God's request, not ours. Despite having suffered five rough attacks of flu that winter, the couple accepted our invitation and boarded a jet in below zero weather for California. Mrs. Billheimer was so frail she had to lie down during much of the flight and attended the week's meetings in a wheelchair. But their health was distinctly improved by the end of the conference.

During this visit to Southern California, the Billheimers appeared on Trinity Broadcasting Network's Praise the Lord Program to discuss their book. Paul Crouch, president of the network, had ordered ten thousand copies to distribute and was enthusiastic about its deep spiritual insights.

While on the air, Paul asked Reverend Billheimer if he would consider a television teaching ministry with the network. Because of his advanced age and frail health, the invitation

seemed unreal. Overwhelmed and reeling,
Reverend Billheimer voiced a feeble consent, cer-
tain that he was dreaming.

But it was no dream. Videotaping began im-
mediately, and the Billheimers soon moved to
California for a full-time television ministry. Now,
after nearly two years on the air, their teaching is
being carried by satellite to many parts of the
globe. Brought out of the dark Georgia woods
into the blinding lights of international television,
the Billheimers are using their talents for God.
Age and ill health have not stopped them from
leading thousands more to the gates of Heaven.

CHAPTER 5

A CITY AMONG THE STARS

It was a sweltering day in Chicago when Dr. Richard Eby fell through a termite-eaten second story wooden balcony railing, plunging headlong to the sidewalk below. His head broken wide open, Dr. Eby's dead body lay crumpled in a pool of blood. But his soul — for a few moments at least — was in Paradise, the "reception room to Heaven."

I marveled as Dr. Eby, a highly respected obstetrician, related to me on his first television appearance the details of his visit to heavenly realms. The story, now told in his book, Caught Up Into Paradise, is one of many describing the beautiful realities of Heaven.[1]

Finding himself living in a new, cloud-like body, Dr. Eby felt peaceful and free from pain. Clothed in a translucent, flowing white gown, he realized the form was his, but that he was transparent. The beautiful flowers and grasses he walked on were undisturbed by his footsteps; air was unnecessary because Jesus provided all the energy and life he needed.

Thinking he would stoop and pick some of the perfectly symmetrical flowers, Dr. Eby discovered no time lag exists between thought and action.

The beauties he beheld were suddenly in his
hands. A land void of shadows, Paradise is illumi-
nated by the brilliant glory of God, and angelic
melodies fill the air; their voices seemed to come
from everywhere at once.

As Dr. Eby marveled at the peace and serene
joy filling his consciousness, he found himself
traveling a narrow path down a long, beautiful
valley. One instant he was weightlessly floating
along, his steps effortless, and the next he found
himself back in his unconscious body imprisoned
on a hospital bed. He had returned.

The Celestial Metropolis

Visions of the "other side" resulting from
death or near-death experiences must always be
weighed against the infallible evidence of God's
Word. Certainly much exists beyond what the
Bible reveals, but God has chosen not to show
most of us these further mysteries until it is our
time to journey beyond. To explore the hidden
realms on our own — through such occult tech-
niques as seances, Ouija boards and astral (out-of-
body) travel — is to invite disaster.

God has given us much information in the
Bible to indicate the incredible wonders of
Heaven. The fullest description is given by the
Apostle John in the Book of Revelation, which
describes the sights he viewed from his island
exile.[2]

John saw the city of New Jerusalem — God's
heavenly capitol — descending from the sky. Full

of God's glory, it sparkled and flashed like a multifaceted diamond, glowing with the purest golden light. Incredibly, this celestial city stretched 1,500 miles in each direction and rose tier upon tier into the sky. Imagine a metropolis stretching northerly from San Diego to Prince George, British Columbia, then over to the south edge of the Hudson Bay, down to Dallas and back to San Diego. Now picture it rising level upon level many times higher than the orbits of today's satellites! That's how large this city in the heavens is.

Without sun or moon to light it, the metropolis is filled with the dazzling glory of God, a vibrating, living light that radiates continually from every being and object. Reflecting and glistening in this white light are the translucent gold structures and the enchanting stone walls, sparkling with precious gems.

Visualize the symphony of colors radiating from the jeweled city walls described by John: Red and yellow play off the green emeralds as topaz blends with the orange jacinth and violet amethyst.

Between the luminous walls and foundations is a city of gold and a main street glowing with a transparent golden hue, smooth as glass. Coursing down the center of the main boulevard is a crystal-clear river, the water of life flowing from the throne of God. The purest mountain stream on Earth is like a stagnant pond by comparison.

Along the river are broad expanses of floral grandeur and Trees of Life, each bearing fruit in

fragrant bloom. Every part of the city is filled
with perfect flowers, trees and grasses, all full of
vibrant life and exquisite fragrance.

No sorrow is found in this heavenly paradise,
for joy is the atmosphere of Heaven. After John
saw the City of God, he could hardly wait to
enter its splendors. "Come, Lord Jesus," he
prayed. The Apostle Paul was so thrilled by his
glimpse of Heaven that he was torn by his desire
to go there and fulfilling his mission on Earth.
Stephen, the martyr, saw such beauty surround-
ing Jesus in the starry metropolis that the pain-
ful pummelling of heavy stones could not wipe
the peaceful smile from his lips.[3]

Glimpses of Paradise

Down through history, God has shown Heaven
to many of His saints. In modern times, He has
allowed others glimpses of the heavenly realms,
which help fill out the picture painted by the
apostles.

General William Booth, founder of the Salva-
tion Army, saw a portion of Heaven which
changed his life. His description echoes that of
Dr. Eby:

> No human eyes ever beheld such per-
> fection, such beauty. No earthly ear
> ever heard such music. No human heart
> ever experienced such ecstasy as it was
> my privilege to see, hear and feel in the
> celestial country.
>
> Around me was an atmosphere so
> balmy that it made my whole frame

vibrate with pleasure. The bank of roses
on which I found myself reposing had,
flowing by it, the waters of the clearest,
purest river that seemed to dance with
delight to its own murmurings.

The trees that grew upon the banks
were covered with the greenest foliage
and laden with the most delicious fruit
— sweet beyond all earthly sweetness —
and by lifting my hand I could pluck
and taste; while in every direction
above and around me the whole air
seemed to be laden with the sweetest
odor coming from the fairest flowers.[4]

As a teenager, Betty Baxter of Albuquerque,
New Mexico, traveled to the other side, where she
was promised healing for her hopelessly twisted
body. As she relates the story of her miraculous
restoration which occurred a few months after
her return, Betty describes the celestial scene
where she walked with Jesus. Here is a brief ex-
cerpt:

"At last we heard music in the dis-
tance, the most beautiful music I had
ever heard. We quickened our steps. We
came to a wide river, separating us from
that beautiful land. I looked on the
other side and saw green grass, flowers
of every color, beautiful flowers that
would never die. I saw the river of life
wending its way through the City of
God."[5]

Thirty Minutes in Heaven

Marvin Ford lay dead in a hospital room for thirty minutes. Transported at incredible speed deep through the blackness of outer space, he was allowed to view the splendors of the holy capital witnessed by John:

"From my vantage point high above the heavenly metropolis, I could see massive jasper walls stretching far into the distance. Surrounding the city, the transparent walls reflected a brilliant yellow-green light, which mingled harmoniously with the multicolored hues of gem-studded foundations. Inset at regular intervals, three on each side of the city, were gates of pearl, each gate a beautiful solid round pearl a hundred or more miles in diameter. Astonishingly, shadows do not exist, for a delicate transparency prevails throughout Heaven . . .

As I drew closer, the walls faded into the distances. Millions of small, sparkling lights came into view, which appeared to be dancing gracefully in perfect harmony, singing melodies more beautiful than man has ever heard. For a moment it seemed I had become one of those lights and joined them in song. I could understand the lyrics of this heavenly tongue.

My attention was attracted toward a dazzling white light radiating from the center of the city. Its brilliance made the other lights pale by comparison ... A huge rainbow arched above the light like a crowning dome ... I saw hues that do not exist on Earth ...

Every house, street, tree, flower, river and mountain in Heaven is the embodiment of this brilliance. Auras of rainbow hues surround every person and angel in the city, so resplendent no mortal can look upon them. Having life-giving properties, the light appears to emanate from the individual, though it is a reflection of the great splendor coming from the center of the city.

... The aura gives one the appearance of being dressed in flawless white, while at the same time clothed in beautiful colors of varied hues."[6]

Fountains and Gardens

Marietta Davis saw Heaven as well as Hell in the nine days she lay in a coma. Escorted by an angel, she also saw the City of God:

"Soon we emerged from the ascending gallery of rainbows and stood upon an aerial plain, resting in the transparent air above the magnificent and lofty dome which crowns the center temple of instruction in the paradisical abode.

From this position I beheld the great city, reaching on every side beneath my view. Majestic trees in groups and at regular intervals arose, bearing a profusion of fragrant and shining clusters of flowers . . .

Fountains of living waters also were visible, some just rising from the green grass, and flowing through their marble channels, or through beds of golden sands, with a low and pleasant murmer; while others gushed forth in full volume to a lofty height, and descended in glowing streams . . .

The entire city appeared one garden of flowers; one grove of umbrage; one undulating sea of fountains; one unbroken extent of sumptuous architecture all set in a surrounding landscape of corresponding beauty, and overarched by a sky adorned with hues of immortal light that bathed and encircled each and every object."[7]

Joyful Reunions

One of the beauties of Heaven will be the joyful reunion of friends and relatives. All tears washed away and sorrows vanquished, we will recognize our loved ones and share the marvels performed by the Lord through our lives on Earth.

Missionary Lorne Fox was rejoined with many he knew from Earth on his visit to Paradise:

"We walked along the winding road-
way into a magnificent garden. I have
seen the flowers of the far north, and
the exquisite flowers of the far south,
but nothing can compare with the color
of flowers that bloom in that eternal
land!

I was walking now, in the paradise
garden within the heart of the kingdom
of Heaven! And it was there that I met
many friends and loved ones, whom I
recognized. My own little mother came
to me, with her hands extended in wel-
come . . . She was perfect, young and
radiant, as are all within those portals."[8]

One who visited Heaven early in this century,
Seneca Sodi, reports meeting a woman whom he
had known on Earth as a hopeless invalid:

"I cannot tell how we recognized each
other, but there is such a similarity of
the spirit itself to the bodily features
that we at once knew each other, and
memory was so fresh that we seemed
never to have forgotten anyone. She
seemed so well now, and her face was
beaming with immortal youth.

Sodi met many others he had known on Earth:

We have to have reunions on Earth,
but they could in no wise compare to
the joy of this meeting. Some of these
had been (in Heaven) for many years.
In a few moments more we were em-
braced in each other's arms. Oh, such

joy I never knew before and such wel-
come!

Among these was my own dear
mother. She had died many years ago.
How she knew me I cannot tell, nor
how I knew her I do not know; but she
rushed toward me, and I knew her so
well and said, "Oh, Mother, is that
you?" She was beautiful and lovely.

She embraced me in her arms and
said, "I knew you were coming." The
memories of childhood and all her
smiles and kindness, which a mother's
love suggests, came back to me. There
were many others like myself: mothers
and sons, fathers and children, old
friends meeting again. The glory and
joy of the occasion excelled anything I
had yet known."[9]

Another who experienced a beyond and back
visit to Heaven was James E. "Johnny" Johnson,
former assistant secretary of the Navy and vice
chairman of the Civil Service Commission. Pro-
nounced dead in a brutal traffic accident,
Johnson was carried to the celestial city before
returning to his body. While there he first met his
dead son, Ken:

I could tell he was talking to me. It
seemed I was trying to talk to him be-
cause I was surprised to see him. He
didn't have on a uniform as he did
when he went to be with the Lord. He
wore a light garment.

It reminded me of when he was baptized ... Ken had on a long white gown. It was so vivid. I felt such a warm glow at the time he walked into the water and was immersed.

I felt the same love, the same warmth. It was as if he were talking to me. And I felt his love.

He said several times the same thing that he had before: 'Take care of Mother. Take care of Mother and the children."

Johnson then saw his father-in-law and his own parents. Although they had never met in earthly life, they stood together, "not as strangers to each other. I could feel the love among them. And all wore the same white clothes."[10]

The Author of Love

Beyond meeting loved ones, the greatest thrill awaiting our entrance into Heaven is meeting the Author of Love, Jesus. Evangelist Kenneth Hagin recalls his visit to the other side:

We came to the throne of God, and I beheld it in all its splendor. I was not able to look upon the face of God, but only beheld His form.

I was first attracted to the rainbow about the throne ...., then to the winged creatures on either side ... They were peculiar looking creatures, and as I walked

up with Jesus, these creatures stood
with wings outstretched. They had
eyes of fire set all the way around their
heads, and they looked in all directions
at once . . .

Then for the first time I actually
looked into the eyes of Jesus. Like
wells of living love, their tender look is
indescribable. As I looked into His
eyes, I fell at His feet."[11]

All the glories of Earth and the splendors of
Heaven pale before the incredible presence of
Jesus.

At times we believe we know what love is,
what it means to give, what joy is all about. We
sensed a fragment of divine happiness when we
first met Jesus, when we experienced heavenly
peace or shared the love of God with someone
else. But to stand face to face with Jesus — to feel
His warm touch, see His smile of loving accept-
ance, to walk with Him through the splendor of
Heaven and hear Him explain with simple clarity
the eternal mysteries of God — all this is the true
glory of Heaven. There, a sweet but irresistible
force of love transcends the most fertile imagina-
tion of the greatest poets Earth has produced. As
the divine spark within us is kindled into a glow-
ing flame, all the fog-enshrouded wonderings of
our present will be burned away; we will "know
even as we are known" by the eternal Christ.[12]

Custom Built Mansions

Unlike Hell, which was made for fallen spirits and only grudgingly accommodates man, Heaven was specifically made for us. "I go to prepare a place for you," Jesus said.[13] With countless angel craftsmen under His command, the Lord has been using His infinite creative power to build a city that will fulfill our wildest dreams of beauty and happiness.

Just think of it: The One who knows our every thought and desire has been supervising construction of a magnificent dwelling just for us! He has taken every measurement into consideration and applied them to the perfect dimensions of our personal mansion. Each pure human desire for beauty, fragrance, music, symmetry, taste and feeling has been meticulously incorporated into the landscape of Heaven.

An infinite variety of flowers and fruit has been planted to entertain the eye and gormandize the palate. Living water is flowing from God's throne, just waiting for you and me to quench our thirst. The warm, golden glow of God's light is bathing every corner of the heavenly city in anticipation of our arrival. Moses, Joshua, Isaiah, John, Paul, and all the great biblical servants of God are bursting with tales of wonder. Our loved ones and ancestors wait to escort us through the splendors of the city and help us explore the dazzling variety of worlds spread throughout the infinite universe. All of this has been put together by a loving God for our pleasure.

Follow Your Heart

While people must work hard to go to Hell, the way to Heaven is natural to man. Instinctively, we reach out for something beyond this life. We sense death is not the end of existence. An inward tug draws us toward our Creator, and no one feels more keenly that he has missed the true purpose of life than the one who has run away from that divine pull.

No one in history, however wise or great, has ever matched the perfection of Jesus. We need only look at a few simple words of this God-man to find the entrance to Heaven:

"I am the way, the truth, and the life: no man cometh unto the Father, but by me."[14]

All of us are born in sin and live in its midst. Nevertheless, Jesus paid the price of admission to Heaven for us:

"God commandeth (showed) His love toward us, in that, while we were yet sinners, Christ died for us."[15]

Accepting His death on our behalf, we enter immediately into eternal life, and upon leaving this body are transported directly to Heaven. The way to Heaven has been prepared; its gates are open wide to those who commit their lives to Christ. Jesus stands with outstretched arms to receive us into splendors that will dazzle our eyes, into beauties that will enchant our senses, and into knowledge that will fascinate our immeasurably expanded minds.

Surpassing Delights

What could be greater than these celestial glories?

Just imagine the joy of walking the celestial streets arm in arm with your family, knowing your persistent prayers had rescued them from the eternal tortures of Hell. The delights of Heaven will be much sweeter as the story is shared among loved ones for eternity.

Wonderful as Heaven is, it will be even more glorious for the Christian worker crowned by God in reward for faithful service.

Radiant as Heaven is, its glow will be brighter for the mother whose pain and sacrifice made it possible for her son to stand with the redeemed before God's throne.

Beautiful as Heaven's music is, its exquisite tones will blend in sweeter harmony for the wife whose faithful devotion helped win the heart of the once rebellious husband who now holds her hand.

Filled with splendors beyond our imagination, Heaven's wonders are freely available to all who are in Christ Jesus. But beyond the glories of Paradise itself are the thrills of bringing others along, sharing together the delights of God's presence and recounting the wonderful stories of how He used us to lead others to eternal bliss.

Broken Chains

With heavy chains tightly wrapped about his head, neck and body, a gruesome figure slipped down the aisle toward the altar of our church.

Ralph Garcia, with his black leather jacket, unwashed hair and scraggly beard, was exactly what he appeared to be: a product straight from the pit of despair.

Praying for his deliverance, I wondered what had driven him to such depths.

The next morning a handsome young man, holding a huge Bible, told me the sordid story. I was at the church early to pray with the choir as it prepared to leave on a tour on our bus. As I entered the crowded bus, a happy voice called, "Pastor Barnard, I want you to meet somebody."

She pointed to a clean-shaven, gentle looking youth. "Do you know who this is?" she smiled.

"No, I don't," I hesitated.

"This is my brother, Ralph!"

Forgetting the sad image of the night before, I was amazed by the drastic change in his appearance. I didn't recognize him.

"I came to your church because she forced me," Ralph grinned, jabbing a thumb in her direction. "I was in chains, but today I am free."

The young man looked into her dark eyes and beamed as he continued. "I once hated my sister. All she ever talked about was Jesus."

His account is one of the most thrilling examples of God's miracle working power I've ever heard.

Ralph's rebellion began when he was eight years old. Coming from a broken home and doing poorly in school, he began running the streets and getting into trouble. His mother's pleas to clean up and take a bath were met with eyes full of such hatred that she feared for her life. Finally moving out of the house, Ralph lived in a filthy chicken coop in the back yard.

His teenage years were filled with drugs, sex, liquor and crime. One day, Ralph picked up a hitchhiker who claimed his name was Damballa. Telling Ralph that he loved and worshiped Satan, Damballa introduced him to the occult. Ralph's revolt deepened as he turned to the devil.

Become fast friends, the two young men formed a motorcycle gang called "Disciples of the Demon's Teachings." Riding their "choppers," the gang held wild drug-hazed parties and brought fear to the community. Damballa gave demonic names to everyone in the group: Enock, Seava, Khancum, Lucifer. Ralph's name was Mosie.

"I never learned to read," Ralph continued. "My sister used to read the Bible to me. While in demon worship, I was haunted by one verse. It was, 'The wages of sin is death; but the gift of God is eternal life through Jesus Christ.' "[16]

Whenever he allowed these words to penetrate the haze of drugs, he was filled with fear and would deal with it by getting "wasted" on drugs and alcohol.

Constant Prayer

Still his sister and mother prayed for him, trusting God to save even someone as defiant as Ralph. Searching for a rock station on his radio one afternoon, he tuned into a Christian program. It was a live service in which the speaker was exorcising a demon from someone in the audience.

"Come out in the name of Jesus!" the preacher commanded. Instantly Ralph was thrown to his knees, roaring like a wounded animal. Scratching and struggling toward the door, he finally escaped that voice of authority on the radio, but he was consumed by gnawing fear from that moment on.

It wasn't long before Ralph and his friends were "busted" by the police for possession of marijuana. While in jail, his days included visits from his family, still telling him of Jesus' love; his nights were restless, accompanied by terrifying nightmares. Upon his release, Ralph was angrier and more unmanageable then before.

Somehow life wasn't the same. Disgusted with himself and his friends, Ralph wondered if there was any hope. His search for happiness led only to despair.

His sister continued her gentle influence, reading to him from the Bible whenever she could persuade him to listen.

"For God so loved the world. that he gave his only begotten Son, that whosoever believeth in him should not perish, but have everlasting life. For

God sent not his Son into the world to condemn the world; but that the world through him might be saved."[17]

"I just couldn't forget those words," Ralph recalled. "I began to feel God touching my heart. Secretly, I held my sister's Bible in my hands and prayed for help."

"No outward change took place," his sister interrupted. "He was still heavily into drugs and even attempted to kill me. But slowly a transformation was occurring inside him."

In response to his sister's constant urging, Ralph decided to go to church with her — just as he was: leather jacket, scraggly beard and hair, wrapped with heavy chains.

It was a Friday night I had set aside for fasting and prayer in our church, believing God for miracles to meet especially difficult needs. When I invited to the front those who wanted help, Ralph came forward, chains and all. Sensing in my spirit that he was demon possessed, I prayed for him as he knelt at the altar, but nothing seemed to happen.

As I continued to pray for others, an inward knowledge came to me from God that a young child in the audience was oppressed by demonic forces. Asking the parents to bring the child, I prayed for his deliverance.

"In Jesus' name, I command you, Satan, to take your hands off this child," I ordered. Suddenly Ralph flew into a rage.

As he lunged toward me, five of our strong men grabbed and forced him down. "It's all or nothing now," I thought, turning my attention to the violent struggle before me.

After nearly thirty minutes of praying for his deliverance, I knew he was free. "Turn him loose," I told the men, and Ralph melted before us like a baby. Tears trickled from his eyes.

"You're free!" I beamed. "Take off your chains."

Smiling, he reached up and removed the chains one by one. Running to us from the audience, his mother and sister threw their arms around him and cried. The powers of Hell were broken, and the hate of twenty years fell away.

Soon after Ralph and his sister recounted these events, he asked God to help him learn to read the Bible, since he couldn't decipher even the simplest sentences. Miraculously, he stood up in church three weeks later and read portions of the Old Testament aloud to the congregation.

Ralph is now an evangelist, and I had the pleasure of performing his wedding to a beautiful young girl. His life is a testimony to the faithfulness of his sister and mother and to the power of prayer. No matter how hopeless the situation seemed, they held on in faith and love, and God answered their prayers. Through prayer and living by God's Word we can miss the agonies of Hell, and attain the wonders of Heaven.

SOURCE NOTES

Chapter 1

[1] Ezek. 3:18-21.

Chapter 2

[1] Richard Wurmbrand, Tortured for Christ (Diane Books, Glendale, Calif., 1969), p.39.

[2] Lorne F. Fox, Visions of Heaven, Hell and the Cross (Privately published, P.O. Box 34, Naselle, Wash.), pp.15-20.

[3] Jean-Baptiste Delacour, Glimpses of the Beyond, trans. by E.B. Garside (Delacorte Press, New York, 1974), p.31.

[4] Richard E. Eby, Caught Up Into Paradise (Richard Eby, P.O. Box 656, Upland, Calif., 1978), pp.229, 230.

[5] George Godkin, adapted from his testimony printed in a privately published leaflet.

[6] Gordon Lindsay, ed., Scenes Beyond the Grave (Christ for the Nations, Dallas, Tex., 1973), pp.61–73.

[7] Kenneth Hagin, adapted from his testimony, "I Went to Hell," printed in a privately published leaflet.

[8] Adapted from Luke 16:19-31.

[9] Heb. 1:7.

[10] Psa. 9:17.

[11] Job 26:5.

[12] II Peter 2:4.

[13] Luke 8:30-33.

[14] Matt. 25:41.

[15] Matt. 12:40.

[16] Luke 10:15.

[17] Prov. 15:24.

[18] Job 26:5, 6; Isa. 28:17.

[19] George Johnson and Don Tanner, The Bible and the Bermuda Triangle (Logos International, Plainfield, N.J., 1976).

[20] Matt. 25:41.

Chapter 3

[1] Prov. 3:19.

[2] Rom. 11:3; I Cor. 1:25.

[3] Rev. 14:11.

[4] Rev. 20:10.

[5] Mark 9:43-48.

[6] Ezra Coppin, Turn Loose (Faith Outreach International, Box 413, San Diego, Calif., 1976).

Chapter 4

[1] Acts 16:25-34.

[2] Acts 9:1-31; 13:9.

[3] Eph. 6:12.

[4] Mark 11:24.

[5] Eph. 5:22-25, 33.

[6] Eph. 5:31.

[7] Prov. 22:6, 23:13, 14.

[8] Matt. 18:19.

Chapter 5

[1] Epy, op. cit.

[2] Rev. 21:10-22:5.

[3] II Cor. 12:2-4; Acts 7:54-60.

[4] H.A. Baker, Heaven and the Angels (Baker Book Concern, 3940 South 24th Ave., Minneapolis, Minn., n.d.), p.63.

[5] Ralph Wilkerson, Beyond and Back (Melodyland Publishers, P.O. Box 6000, Anaheim, Calif., 1977). p.108.

[6] Marvin Ford, as told to Dave Balsiger and Don Tanner, On the Other Side (Logos International, Plainfield, N.J., 1978), pp.159, 166.

[7] Lindsay, op.cit., pp.52-54.

[8] Fox, op.cit., pp.25,26.

[9] Elwood Scott, Paradise: The City and Throne (Privately published, 1909), pp.33,34.

[10] James E. Johnson, with David W. Balsiger, <u>Beyond Defeat</u> (Doubleday Galilee Books, New York, 1978), p.263.

[11] Kenneth Hagin <u>I Believe in Visions</u> (Fleming H. Revell, Old Tappan, N.J., 1972), pp.48, 50.

[12] I Cor. 13:12.

[13] John 14:2.

[14] John 14:6.

[15] Rom. 5:8.

[16] Rom. 6:23.

[17] John 3:16, 17.